Gracious Walk

The Path that Leads to Purpose and Fulfillment

RAYMOND PEEPLES

Publisher's Cataloging-In-Publication Data
(Prepared by The Donohue Group, Inc.)

Names: Peeples, Raymond, author.
Title: Gracious walk : the path that leads to purpose and fulfillment / Raymond Peeples.
Description: Cleveland, TN : Deeper Revelation Books, [2019] | Scripture quotations taken from The Holy Bible New International Version and the New King James Version. | Includes bibliographical references.
Identifiers: ISBN 9781949297119
Subjects: LCSH: Peeples, Raymond--Religion. | African American clergy--United States--Biography. | Christian life. | Self-actualization (Psychology)--Religious aspects--Christianity. | God (Christianity)--Worship and love. | LCGFT: Autobiographies. | BISAC: RELIGION / Christian Living / Personal Memoirs.
Classification: LCC BX8765.5.Z8 P44 2019 | DDC 289.94092--dc23

Individuals and church groups may order books from Raymond Peeples directly, or from the publisher. Retailers and wholesalers should order from our distributors. Refer to the Deeper Revelation Books website for distribution information, as well as an online catalog of all our books.

Published by:
Deeper Revelation Books
Revealing "the deep things of God" (1 Cor. 2:10)
P.O. Box 4260
Cleveland, TN 37320 423-478-2843
Website: www.deeperrevelationbooks.org
Email: info@deeperrevelationbooks.org

Deeper Revelation Books assists Christian authors in publishing and distributing their books. Final responsibility for design, content, permissions, editorial accuracy, and doctrinal views, either expressed or implied, belongs to the author.

Table of Contents

Am I a Taker? 15

Changing One's Self – Spirituality 21

Changing One's Self – Loneliness 27

A Letter to Mom and Auntie Deb 33

When the Lord Stops You 49

A Cross in the Picture 51

Can I Be Vulnerable (For the Fellas)? 53

Be Steadfast in Faith and Keep Holding On 57

Had My Dad Told Me, Just Maybe 63

Cultural Acceptance 69

This Mercy Thing Is Confusing 71

Just Grab a Seat and Peddle 75

Let Me Close My Mouth 79

Are You Listening for the Voice of God? 83

Break Every Chain That Holds You 87

God Doesn't Hate You or Me 89

Are We Detrimental in Our Relationships
  Just Being Ourselves? 93

The Lord Can Change You; I'm Proof 97

Angry 101

Saved by Grace 105

A Crazy "Dead People" Dream 111

The Lord Is Working 115

Power of Prayer 119

The Lord Takes Care of His Own 121

A Personal Relationship with Jesus 125

Serving in Church 129

Trust Him and His Promises 133

A Blessed Day Indeed! 137

Always Wear the Armor of God 143

Opportunities to Share the Good News 147
Inspirational Thoughts 151
Acts of Random Kindness (ARK) 161
Be a Blessing! – Thanksgiving Idea 161
Be a Blessing! – Christmas Idea 161
Be a Blessing! – Easter Idea 162
Be a Blessing! – Who Needs You Today 162
Be a Blessing! – Three Difficult Days Each Year ... 163
Be a Blessing! – Setting Right Priorities 163
Be a Blessing! – Easy Blessing Opportunities 163
Be a Blessing! – Server at Church 164
Be a Blessing! – Dementia and Alzheimer's 165
Blessing Awareness! – Let Him Be Him 165
Blessing Awareness! – Let Her Be Her 165
Works Cited 167

Dedication

∽

I dedicate this book to my wife Bibi and our children (Marnier, Aneeza, Kyle, Zameena and Shakeera). I may not always be the perfect dad, but you are all the best things that have ever happened in my life. I also humble myself and thank my Lord Jesus Christ who has always been there for me, even when I was not searching for Him or following Him.

I also need to thank Ally, Annie, Jorge, Earlene, Elbert, Ket, Nicole, Ordella, Patty, and a number of amazing pastors whom I have the opportunity to work with and learn from. You are all blessings in my life.

Foreword

I cannot recall the year, nor month or day that I met Ray Peeples; and yet the occasion is burned into my head like an engraving on a leather purse. I was teaching a class on the subject of hermeneutics (*How to Study the Bible* / because I had pulled the short straw that semester). Most people who take hermeneutics do so because they are compelled by requirements of some sort. Let's be honest: they think the course is a glorified study in grammar. But I was determined to make this class interesting, so I did what all lovers of the Word of God do ... I started combining theology and doctrine with the lessons.

This is where Ray comes in. He sat quietly in the back of the class making no fuss or disturbance whatsoever, which is a really nice way to say that I hardly noticed him. It took one sentence and less than one minute for that to change forever. I and my co-teacher thought it would be great one evening to study Scripture pertaining to water baptism. We had barely completed what I thought was an astounding lecture/class discussion on John 1:29–33 when "Mr. Quiet" in the back of the room raises his hand and says, "I am not so sure about water baptism." I am not wanting to start a debate or even a discussion on the topic. Just know that for me, he may as well have slapped my face with a glove filled with gravel! I halted all further discussions and lectures because we needed to help this confused young man … immediately. I stopped teaching and started preaching, I am pretty sure I preached right through the break. To his credit, he sat there listening quietly and politely. But still he questioned everything, and I mean everything I had said to him.

I left that night knowing I had some serious praying to do and it was all for Ray. I accepted in my heart that it might take weeks, but I trusted in the Lord to change Ray's heart.

Less than 24 hours later, I looked up at the baptismal pool and there he was, getting baptized! Did my words change his thinking? I doubt it. Radical change like that requires a move of God. I believe that God pulled Ray into His Presence and convicted him on the subject. Conviction happens to believers/true believers. The author of this book is a man who is chasing God! His desire to be in the presence and the will of the Lord is paramount above all else that can be said about him. He is genuine to his core, and I am not trying to make a saint here, but to simply reflect his basic nature. He serves God in any way that he is called to do, and he does so humbly. I am quite honored to know this man who is consistently generous in time, talent and finances and always has a kind word for a stranger (any stranger, maybe all strangers).

Knowing that *Gracious Walk* is written by a man of God, you may be thinking of him in terms of other men of God that you know or have met. You may be thinking that this is just another Christian feel-good book. Please stop that right now. Ray is a man, an American man, which means he is/was challenged in many cultural beliefs with respect to women and most definitely to male behavior. This is a chronicle, if you will, of his growth away from some of the cultural norms, which are harmful to us as a society and as individuals. Ray takes real life situations, challenges, failures, and triumphs, and through incredible transparency, reveals what most of use try desperately to hide: that God is or wants to be a part of every aspect of our lives.

Ray opens up in a way that most men fear to do. Not so many women open up this much either. The transparency of *Gracious Walk* taps into the practical applications of the Word. There is in each of us a vulnerable person who needs to know that not only is he or she not alone, but that there is an answer. *Gracious Walk* is Ray Peeples contribution to the maturing mindset of our society: a society that is kinder, more considerate, more generous and loving, but most of all … more Christ-like.

– Pastor Caryl Patterson

Introduction

∽

This book is the result of having someone speaking it into my life, the same person who spoke attending ministry school into my life. Today, I'm still blown away that I'm a pastor. Although, I will tell you right up front, I'm not your typical pastor. I make no apologies for the blessings of the Lord. All praise, glory, and thanks to Him for everything He does and how I've been blessed. Additional thanks for all the godly people who surround me, hold me accountable for my actions, praying constantly for me and those whom I have the humble honor to surround and pray for.

The Gospel ownership is not a me thing; it is an us thing. We each own the sharing about the good news of Jesus Christ and the Word of God (the Bible). We each have an earthly assignment and need to meet people where they are in life. As the apostle Paul wrote, *"To the weak became I as weak, that I might gain the weak: I am made all things to all men, that I might by all means save some. And this I do for the gospel's sake, that I might be partaker thereof with you"* (1 Corinthians 9:22-23).

Allow me to share a recent text conversation with one of my friends from church. Per Cindy, *"I think you are very good at connecting with people and have a very good heart. You are very intelligent and can read people pretty good from what I can tell. I'm not sure I think of "Minister" when I think of you, but that's my crazy opinion. Maybe I hold ministers up to be more than human. I never would have guessed you were so serious about becoming a licensed minister. Go figure … I do hope God uses you to do great and mighty things, and you get all the desires of your heart. You will always be my friend no matter what."* My response, *"It wasn't my idea. A friend spoke it into my life."* I was content just being a blessing and helping others.

She called one day and asked me when I was going – told her I wasn't. A few months later she asked again and I spoke with Pastor Chuck about local schools, and he told me about Faith Assembly's Ministry Program. A week later I was in school. Pastor Caryl was my first instructor. I'm not thinking of leaving my job, but the Lord could have a different plan. We will see. It is okay people don't see me as a Pastor. Most are surprised when they hear it. I'm clearly not typical. I don't always follow the rules." Cindy then says, *"LOL! Well it will sure be interesting to see where the Lord leads you. You are most definitely not a typical minister type. Too much class and style. Your taste for fine suits, four-star restaurants, and high-end living does not necessarily line up with a typical minister. At least any that I know, but then again what do I know? I'm glad I'm along for the ride! Please forgive my sense of humor at a time like this. I honestly don't want to offend you either. I promise to be one of your biggest supporters whatever happens, but I say, 'Go God Go!' He has recruited some pretty odd characters in the past and made them great ministers indeed."*

This text conversation was an interesting dialogue, but what you'll be reading in this book are my past struggles and how over a period of time, my life changed. I've made countless mistakes, multiple times, but our Lord is forgiving and faithful. He can turn any situation around and use us beyond our wildest dreams and imagined thoughts. We all have experienced or will experience difficulties in this short period of time that we will spend on earth. A time of joy, happiness, sadness, struggles, and pains, but we are not bound to it. Yet, we have a shelter, place of comfort, peace, wisdom, guidance, and unwavering love, a love that our Lord Jesus Christ offers to each and every one of us. We really don't like anyone telling us how we should live our lives. The most difficult part for many will be accepting what is placed before us in the Bible (i.e. *Basic Instructions Before Leaving Earth*).

I will be the first to tell you, "I have a blessed life," but it is all due to the blessing of our God, His Son Jesus Christ, and the Holy Spirit who resides in me. Nothing I have or have achieved was without Him. Besides, it is all temporal and on loan to me. I pray that I am a good steward of it all. This you might find interesting. I struggled for days with writing this introduction. Not until one morning around 4:00am did it come together after praying upon my knees.

Thank you, Lord, for everything. I pray the Lord guides you and that you find yourself uplifted in the letters and inspirational messages I've written over the years. May God bless you, your families, and your friends. At the end of the day or I should say, *"By the time you get to the final page, I hope this book will have enlightened and inspired you to keep trusting, believing, and walking with God. May you find enlightenment and inspiration as you read through these pages of the book which is a glimpse into my life."*

CHAPTER 1

Am I a Taker?

At what point do people realize they are *takers* and not *givers?* Historically we have been told, it is better to give than receive, and let's be honest, receiving is really good. Our parents and grandparents, if it was within their means, showered us with love and gifts. So, for the sake of argument, let us just agree, receiving is good and doesn't require effort for the *taker*, but lots of effort and energy for the *giver.* So, fast forward into my personal assessment. I realize painfully I have been a *taker.* Not from the perspective of gifts, although I will accept them with a smile, but a *taker* in the form of "I." I want to do this, I don't want to watch this, I want to see this movie. I, I, I, I and a few more I's for the things I'm sure I intentionally left out. It was truly all about me.

I recognize now that the "all about me" mentality has history dating back to my late twenties after my first heart break. Neither Dad nor any close brothers from the hood talked about the emotional side of getting hurt. As of today, I don't have a single male friend who I have ever publicly heard say he was hurt. Someone gets burned once or twice and anyone coming after that is potentially doomed. I have met and dated some of the most amazing, brilliant, and beautiful women ever from around the world (United States, South America, Africa, Japan, Italy, and Laos). But the moment they appeared to do something that reminded me of the past, it was war or the immediate exit (I'm outta here). How stupid was that! Anyone trying to advance up my unconditional love hill faced boulders, holes with sharp stakes, booby traps, and land mines. I'm sure as a reader of this you cannot relate. And the most luminous act of all, if the other stuff didn't work, I'd just stop talking. That was 'brilliance' at its best.

It was all about me, how to protect myself at all costs and ensure my happiness. If she gave me leeway with this approach, I'd take off running and never look back. Eventually, I suspect they began to feel unfulfilled, alone, and left out of my life. But, from my perspective, our relationship was wonderful. I honestly couldn't see the problem. From my view, I'm participating. She seemed happy with the things I planned, but never did I ask, *"Babe, what do you want to do? Is there anything you need, or how can I help you?"* Let me be clear, I have cracked the door to my heart. But as soon as the battle started, I went into lock down, just like being in prison. It's not funny how quickly we remember relationship pains. The right music, the right smell in the air, or even a gesture or verbal word can trigger a disastrous response. Past hurts can have horrendous effects on future relationships. Our must-have relationship check list and its unbeknownst timing (our internal, secret, relationship schedule) sets immediate hurdles to jump for that interested person.

I read a book by Dr. Gary Chapman called, *The Five Love Languages* ("Acts of Service, Quality Time, Words of Affirmation, Physical Touch, and Gifts"). It had never dawned on me that

Past hurts can have horrendous effects on future relationships.

maybe I wasn't giving the right thing. In my head, I thought everyone liked gifts. So, I would go about my little merry way buying gifts and giving them. I never imagined, nor had anyone suggested, that maybe the love language I was speaking was incorrect. I just assumed if their response was interpreted as lukewarm, or not as I expected in my mind, I didn't try it again. It made it so easy to just focus on me. So, one of my love languages is words of affirmation, essentially validation that I have done something correct. Like a trained dog being given a reward, if this had happened, I probably would have continued giving. Ok, so I'm dumb, apologetic, and humbled, but I get it now and changes are abounding.

Burying the "all about me mentality," I've set up a series of digital daily reminders. I've heard that words spoken become reality. So, I state aloud each day, *"It's not all about me. I choose to be a giver this day, not a taker."* I also make daily deposits into others' relational vault. Meaning, I strive every single day to give a nice compliment, offer a leading hand, offer a compassionate ear, and pay close attention *not* to think or act in terms of the "all about me" mentality.

Some might say a relational deposit is just an excuse for me to flirt, and yes, I admit, flirting has been a problem for me in my past. I didn't always know the boundary lines, and I recognize my faults and failures. Today, I just make the deposit into another's life and show no other attracted interest. Thus, I've experienced some amazing results and feelings from the act of kindness. The most important thing I have learned is to forgive myself and anyone that ever hurt me. We, yes that includes you, must remove the defensive hurdles and let others see our beautiful character. We must learn to listen with attention and hear with compassion.

~\/~

INSPIRATIONAL THOUGHT

Hold Me Accountable

Rebuke me if I lie. Rebuke me if you hear me use a racial slur. Rebuke me if I'm causing civil unrest and being divisive with my words or behavior. Why? Because this is not who I am, nor should it be a description of anyone I admire, or align myself with, or stand in close proximity to. If you don't, then you must be okay with how I'm acting. Then came Peter to him, and said, *"Lord, how oft shall my brother sin against me, and I forgive him? till seven times"* (Matthew 18:21)?

> *"Blessed is the man whom thou chastenest, O LORD, and teachest him out of thy law"* (Psalms 94:12).

CHAPTER 2

Changing One's Self – Spirituality

I like many others, have discovered or searched for spirituality at different times. My search wasn't the result of addiction or a recent stint in jail. My search should have started in 2008 when I met a woman and constantly heard the song, "Heaven Sent" by Keyshia Cole. I have to proclaim that this woman was truly beautiful inside and out. She was full of life, attractive, intelligent, a great mother, and as my cousin Nicole had told me at the time, *"She could hold her own."*

Let me not forget, her daughter was brilliant in her own right and years beyond her age. But, the man in me was indifferent, working through the "all about me mentality." Some personality traits just do not change overnight. It takes time, and indeed, it took a lot of time for me to change. Back in 2008, when we were dating, she was on my mind constantly. Whenever I was lonely or dealing with a situation, the song would play on a radio. It brought me comfort and peace but didn't change my behavior. I can't say it was, or was not a sign from above, but it always seemed to have played during my life's low period.

By 2010 the relationship was over. She rightly walked away, and it was truly traumatic. As we both know, when something traumatic happens in our lives, we begin to search for solace and peace. Some fall into deep despair, resulting in drugs or alcohol use. In my case, I didn't know what to do. For months I wandered around like a lost dog unable to find its way home. I signed up for online dating, which went nowhere. It was just work and running down to the local pub to hang out with a bunch of Rochester, Michigan friends who gathered to chat and listen to music from the jukebox. It was such a happy period in my life. The only real sources of excitement were my kids and the weekly movies, or shopping with my mom on Saturdays. One day, I will have to talk about how spending every Saturday with one's mom can also have a detrimental effect on their relationship, but that's another story.

My girlfriend decided to end the relationship in January 2010, but it was not until April 2nd, 2010, that I finally found what I needed most in my life. I found the Lord Jesus Christ. It was a strange day. From the moment I aroused from bed that day, the world was out of sync. Everything around me felt weird, but I didn't understand why. Imagine sensing something was different and out of the ordinary, but unable to place a finger on it. I had breakfast, spent time at Knapp's Donut Shop, and then decided to head home. Driving there, I got to the corner of Rochester and Romeo Road. There in front of me loomed St. Phillips Episcopal Church, a church I had passed hundreds of times after moving to Rochester in 1999.

Without hesitation, I pulled into the parking lot, jumped out of the car, and headed inside. Off to GOD's house I trotted, as do many in time of crisis. I was hoping to say a couple of quick "Hail Marys" and a few repeated "Lord's Prayers," ask for forgiveness, get blessed, find peace, and get on

Ask for forgiveness, get blessed, find peace, and get on with life.

with life and my day. I walked into the sanctuary, and there was a man playing the organ. I sat in the very back pew. I wasn't staying long and seeing him there ensured my stay would be short and quick. But that wasn't God's plan. The man said, "I'll let you be alone," and he walked out. I began to pray and cry. I don't remember how long I was there, but when I walked out, my life from that moment has never been the same. For weeks after that, I attended the service there on Sunday mornings—until one day I felt the urge to attend Woodside Bible down the road where I remained until I moved to Florida.

After my contract ended in December of 2010, I didn't have the desire to go to the bar every Friday and Saturday night. Though I had been divorced for many years, I had my kids around and the comfort of my community. I had the feeling that if I wanted companionship, it was all within a 30-minute drive. I also began to realize that insecurity still drove my behavior. At night, I slept with a TV on which provided comfort. If my kids were away, not only would the TV be on, but I always had a light on. I guess that made me, at the time, a forty-year-old who was scared of the dark. Okay, so being open kimono, I still sleep with the TV on. I like the constant noise, and since I don't have a wife to snuggle with, it is companionship.

~࿇~

PRAYER

Relationship Built upon a Strong Foundation

Father, good morning! I praise, honor, and offer up my wholehearted worship. You are worthy to be praised. Lord, I send up prayers for medical healing. Touch the head of those dealing with slowing minds; let us who are around them show them the love they once showed us. I ask You to bind and heal broken hearts. Help us forgive and love again, to comfort those who are still dealing with a loss of a loved one. Get young women's hearts and minds ready for the godly husband You are sending their way. Strengthen the foundation of those recently married and those fighting to stay married. May their marriages be upon the strong foundation of Jesus Christ. Father, I pray they hear and answer Your call upon their hearts. Lord, I thank You for the blessings, mercy, and forgiveness You've given us all. Lord, help us stay prayerful and feel Your presence always. Amen, Amen, and Amen.

> *"I will extol thee, my God, O king; and I will bless thy name for ever and ever. Every day will I bless thee; and I will praise thy name for ever and ever. Great is the Lord, and greatly to be praised; and his greatness is unsearchable"* (Psalms 145:1-3).

CHAPTER 3

Changing One's Self – Loneliness

L et me just say and excuse my foul language, but loneliness is a real 'expletive.' For those of you who know me, you're probably wondering how that can be. He has family, friends, always on the go, so how can he experience being lonely? I would suggest it is easier than you think. It will wake you up in the middle of the night and have you thinking all kinds of thoughts. If you're around people or family and don't feel connected to anyone, you can feel a loneliness inside, that feeling like you don't belong to anyone or they don't belong to you, not in the sense of ownership, but a loving connection. For some, I suspect the feel is temporary, and for others it can last a lifetime. Trust me when I say, loneliness as an insecurity is tough to deal with. Let me put this in context for you. Whenever I hear or even write that word, I have a small panic attack. I have a feeling like a hole in the middle of my chest. It is the same feeling I'm having right now — tight chest and shaking.

Let me share some history about a pivotal period

in my life. I lived in Benton Harbor, Michigan, for about a year, from 2009 to 2010. On Monday mornings, I would drive three hours from my home to the other side of the state to work. This was during the financial crises and folks took employment anywhere they could get it. Hundreds of thousands were being laid off each month, but I would get contracts. The Lord had His hand on my life. So, three nights out of every week I would sit in a hotel room from around 5:30 pm until 6:00 am the next morning. I sat at a desk surfing the net, chatted on Yahoo and watched TV. Talk about being alone. I didn't feel comfortable to call anyone to talk. I didn't want to take their time away from their families to keep me company.

I worked four days a week, and on Thursday afternoons I couldn't get on the road fast enough to get home. I had a strong desire to just get to my house and scream, "I'm home!" and then head to a bar. Yes, the bar, someplace with lots of people.

For months I spent time learning to relax and not letting the loneliness consume me. To be able to sit at home and not have a day filled with activities was a real struggle for me. I historically would have my Saturdays and Sundays filled with activities (i.e. breakfast, movies, shopping, visiting nursing homes, etc.), from the time the sun rose until sunset. The first four months it was really, really hard. I still had breakfast with my mom on Saturday's, but instead of running the streets wildly trying to fill the day, eventually, I returned home by noon. Prior to the change, my Saturdays with Mom and kids started around 7:00 am and didn't end until 7:00 pm.

Those initial months I thought I was going to go crazy. I read. I walked. I surfed the net, but I was having terrible panic attacks and feeling levels of loneliness I cannot describe. So, as I worked through the ability to relax, I began to understand my loneliness issues.

With much bashfulness I admit, that is probably why I like to cuddle and spoon. Yes, I said it. I'm a spooner and I'm okay with the bashing I'm expecting from my brothers. I don't know about you, but I find that cuddling not only connects me with my partner, but I don't feel alone. In times like that, before my divorce, I was able to share with my wife all my insecurities and dreams. Yet, being a spooner has issues, too. How can I cuddle and spoon and still be manly? Can anything just be easy?

I've been reading, *The Blueprint - A Plan for Living Above Life's Storm,* by Kirk Franklin. He makes a remarkable statement, *"So we see the fruit that loneliness bears: bad choices, bad attitudes, cold hearts, lowered standards, destructive cycles – emotional and physical"* (Franklin, 88). I'm able to pick items out of Kirk's list that has impacted my life, but now I accept it as an insecurity, an insecurity that is still a part of my life. But I don't have the bar tendencies any longer and can sit myself down for hours with nothing to do. Can you imagine years of feeling like my day had to be in constant movement and now realizing it doesn't.

You'll have fun with this. One day many years ago, I walked down to a little pond by my house and sat down to reflect. Within moments I started feeling lonely. I looked up and prayed for calmness. All of a sudden, I was no longer alone. Three deer walked out of the woods and sat on the other side of the pond. I just laughed and said, "Thanks." Later that same week, I went back and sat down. Before I even got a chance to feel alone, the same three deer showed up. I shook my head, waived hello, and gave thanks again to the Lord.

Today, I'm in a very weird place in my life. I still have moments of loneliness, but I fill those times with prayer (thanks Anne for the suggestion) and fellowship on Sundays. I have bouts of joy and giving, enhanced thoughts, a renewed sense of integrity, and ownership for respecting others. So, I ask each of you to take a moment and check on the people around you. Maybe they are feeling lonely and could use your compassion right now. Maybe you need to place a carryout order for some cuddling and spooning today with your loved one.

～ﬢﬣ～

PRAYER

I'm Not Going to Worry

Father God, thank You for another day, a day to fellowship with other Christ-minded people. Father, Your Word is clear, Your Word is truthful; we can believe in it 100%. Father, this morning I will not worry. I will not stress; I will not try to "figure it out." I will pray for others, serve others, and trust in You. Father, I pray for all those who are going through a storm or a situation they don't understand. I ask You bring peace to their minds and hearts. Amen, Amen, and Amen.

Not once does the Bible say, *"Worry about it, stress over it, or figure it out."* It says, *"Trust God."*

CHAPTER 4

A Letter to Mom and Auntie Deb

It is funny how things can change over time from a single event, or a series of unexpected events in someone's life. Little would I have expected my life to change as it has since October 2009. At that time, I was dating Ms. K, and we were having all types of difficulties in our relationship. These difficulties spanned a range of things which included not being able to communicate, differences in child rearing (although never discussed), my lack of verbally committing (I thought it was unspoken), lack of quality time, her being a priority in my life, and even the misunderstanding of each other's kids.

Noticing the increasing struggles and prior to the relationship ending in 2010, I had already begun the process of trying to learn how to have a more productive relationship. Not only with her, but also her child. I don't know how many books I read or relationship assessment tests I took. It was countless, yet educational. I really began to understand some of the gaps we faced, and it opened my eyes to other relationships that had previously failed. I read all types of relationship books on being a stepparent even though we were not married. Ms. K at the time had suggested ways to build a relationship with her daughter, but nothing seemed to work. It was truly frustrating. When I did try her recommendations, her daughter's responses didn't give me the impression it was working, so I would start and stop. That on-again and off-again process probably wasn't overly beneficial for the daughter either.

In October of 2009, Ms. K and I had a really good open conversation, and it was an eye-opening moment for me. She laid out exactly what she needed from me and how my overall behavior affected her. What I had assessed through the readings about my behavior was validated by what she was saying. So, I began to change my behavior by doing the things I did when we started dating. I would go to her home on Saturdays instead of spending them with my mom and squeezing her in. Clearly, I began to recognize that she had been giving much more than I was. It was still about the "me" mentality and not much of an "us" mentality. It was kind of like that song, *When Somebody Loves You Back*, by Teddy Pendergrass, the line that says, *"I've experienced over and over again, when I've given 80 percent and she's given 20 percent. Now she's givin' 70 percent and I'm givin' 30."* There was just one slight issue, I never gave more than the minimum.

Things appeared to still be shaky through October and even through till Christmas 2009, but it all collapsed right after the holidays. I suspect the biggest disappointment was that I didn't see her family on Christmas or even before they left. She had said numerous times that she was in a different place mentally, so I gave her space to work through whatever she needed to deal with. Instead of me looking for ways to bridge and address her thoughts, I stayed away and only visited occasionally. By March, she informed me we were officially done. Yep, a true heart break that hurt for a considerable amount of time, but something else was going on which I didn't understand at the time. That day, I placed a stake in the ground to work toward being a better person and make improvements that were way overdue.

> *That day, I placed a stake in the ground to work toward being a better person.*

I recognized that much of what happened in that relationship, as with others, was the result of me. I needed to change. I tried the church thing to understand if maybe it was a spiritual side of me that was missing, but I recognized that the sacramental processes within the churches (Episcopal or Catholic) I was attending didn't make me comfortable and still didn't address what I thought I needed to work on. I knew that the Lord had begun to change me, but the church I was attending didn't provide the nourishment that I needed. It wasn't the lack of the Gospel, but how it was being presented. Thus, I changed churches to a non-denominational one, and the spiritual explosion began.

Sometime in March, while I was in downtown Detroit at a local restaurant called Flood's Bar and Grill, I met this lady from California through an extremely weird circumstance. I was sitting alone at a table, waiting to meet up with my buddy Norman. She just walked over, sat down, and started talking. I eventually met her friends, and we all hung out for hours that evening. Yes, I was being unsafe and offered her a ride home. For some strange reason, I felt the need to show her were I lived as a child in Detroit. I have no clue to this day why I took her by my old home on St. Clair Street. It wasn't as if the house was even noticeable anymore. It was literally surrounded by a forest of weeds and trees. Abandoned to the elements and time, I knew that one day it would cave in and be forever gone. During an hour drive to where she was staying, I learned that she was an avid reader. She ended up recommending several books for me to read just after a few short conversations.

I eventually began to see her as a muse. A muse is someone that motivates and encourages you. The first book she recommended was the *5 Love Languages* by Gary Chapman. That book was interesting because it talked about how people feel love in different ways. The different types were "Quality Time," "Physical Touch," "Words of Affirmation" (appreciation type comments), "Acts of Service" (doing something for them), and "Receiving Gifts." I didn't really realize that "Words of Affirmation" were so important to me in a relationship until I started thinking back over the ones I have had in my past. I also realized that "Physical Touch" was also important, but not from an intimacy perspective, but the realization I was a hugger and spooner. I enjoy a good old-fashion hug. I think because it reminds me that my grandfather, Israel Peeples, was a hugger. As soon as I entered into his presence, he would hug me and run his sandpaper beard against my skin. It was indeed a horrible experience, but I enjoyed it immensely.

I remembered, the days when I thought Ms. K loved me were when she would kiss my forehead. Yes, I know that it's weird, but again, I looked back over other relationships and sure enough, those were my high points. I looked at the people who I've dated and tried to put them into categories based on one of the books I read, and it was interesting. Not sure if the relationships failed because my love language wasn't being fulfilled, but more likely, theirs wasn't, and neither was mine. Back in those days, my servant's heart was just being developed, and I probably wasn't good for anyone.

When I look back over my dating years prior to and including 2009, each of the ladies that I had a long-term relationship with had one thing in common, per what each said or alluded to. They needed or wanted "Quality Time." Yet what I gave were gifts and occasional time. I was giving gifts, which

I thought in my head was showing them love. Yes, today I still like giving a gift, but I do it now as just a gesture of kindness and appreciation, with the real underlying motive, heartfelt admiration. Also, the fact that I like shopping and think I have amazing taste in women's clothing is a plus.

The next book my interim Muse suggested was something about *"How to Have a Perfect Relationship Guaranteed,"* but it was very theoretical and not really a great read. I had also recently started watching Joel Osteen on television on Sunday mornings and talking with my buddy, Deb, from the donut shop about the show when we would meet for coffee. I'm not sure when, but someone recommended one of his books. For almost two months, I kept thinking about getting the book and I didn't. I just kept watching the show and trying to implement some of the things Joel was suggesting.

The first Joel Osteen book I read was *Become a Better You.* It was truly eye-opening experience for me. It talked a lot about how God has a plan for each of us. The book suggested ways to become a better person (in line with my March stake in the ground) and to do more for others than I do for myself. He also discussed how to have a better relationship with your kids through motivation, encouragement, and other things which I didn't doubt needed some improvements.

There is an abundance of blessings awaiting each of us.

It also talked about understanding that there is an abundance of blessings awaiting each of us and the power of prayer. I was already prayerful, but I prayed for tiny things, not thinking in terms of making big prayers.

For instance, I would pray that I wanted to have the ability to make good choices and wise decisions. Or, I would pray for the ability to do lots of little things for others, so that when I leave it would have totaled up to something big. I even prayed that Ms. K and her daughter would return to my life so that I could do the right things by them, but clearly, I wasn't ready. I would pray small things like that, which I thought were small in nature. Little did I know at the time the strange occurrences that would start as I headed on my journey, as I refer to it today.

As I look back over things that have happened in my life, there had been many occurrences of blessing. Besides the kids, I was able to build a house. I had my health and stayed employed during the worse economic depression in my lifetime at the time. If you look at just the employment portion, I was continually able to find employment, and hundreds of thousands were being laid off monthly. The longest gap I was ever unemployed during that time was only one month. The whole time people kept telling me I was blessed. I would always respond humbly that I was lucky.

It really started getting strange when I started going above and beyond for others. I would do almost any activity to be a blessing in someone else's life. Cooking extra food on Sunday to distribute, helping a friend in need, passing out clothes, or giving gift cards, it didn't matter. I was determined to be a blessing and do more for others than I did for myself. Right around that time, I began to see these amazing blessings happening.

- Marnier (my daughter) and Chantel (my niece) got tickets to see Taylor Swift. Okay, my sister Lisa brought the tickets for both shows. But then the second night, they got to actually meet her. Maybe it was just coincidental.

- My mother decided both my kids needed laptops. Maybe this was just coincidental and not the result of anything I had done.

- I got hired at Ford Motor Company while I was concurrently interviewing for a position in Nebraska at Amazon. OKAY, so I thought at the time, I'm trying to learn to be a better me, so why Lord send me back to the place (Ford) where I met Ms. K? She would probably hurt my feelings and remind me that I let her down. I never got an answer, but I was employed.

By the time I returned to Ford, I had completed two of Joel's book and I had really noticed a change in who I was, a change that I have been able to keep in place. I've watched the changes continue to grow through the years.

- I started trying to build a different type of relationship with Kyle and Marnier.

- I started keeping digital notes of what I've learned, and the things that I need to focus on.

- As much as I like to believe otherwise, the world did not revolve around me. What a strange concept! Go figure. I used to think and say, "It is my world, and everyone else is just visiting." I was wrong.

Yea, I still fail at times, but it has changed. One example was the last time I was at the Original House of Pancakes. I normally request a table, and this time Marnier requested one. We ended up sitting in a booth. As a rush of anger started boiling, I thought this was all about me and addressed it quickly. Marnier was frowning, and eventually noticed that I wasn't getting mad, and it didn't even bother me.

Every day I'm getting more comfortable with words of encouragement to both Kyle and Marnier, which has in the past been very difficult. I just needed to stop overthinking and worrying about being perfectly correct when talking with my kids. The funny part is that my personality has changed (which has been very

I get up every morning and start my day by saying, "Yesterday was a good day, but today will be even better."

interesting to watch). I've always been a rather happy person, but I think it was mostly due to my thinking the world revolved around me. Today, I have a different perspective. I get up every morning and start my day by saying, "Yesterday was a good day, but today will be even better."

I've heard numerous pastors suggest that our prayers should be bold and large. I realized that isn't the approach for me. We have to find what works for us in our spiritual prayer life. I now follow what my heart says and not so much what my mind suggests. Yep, it can be a strange event, but I've followed it anyway. So you might say, "Oh, he is finally over Ms. K." Nope, that would not be totally accurate, given that I sent her two of the books that I read. Nope, I never got a thank you, but that's okay. She didn't ask for them, and it was what my heart suggested I do. It goes to doing more for others, regardless if they are accepting. The Bible says we are to continually walk in love, being guided by love, and following love. When God puts love and compassion in your heart towards someone, he's offering you an opportunity to make a difference in that person's life. You must learn to follow that love. Don't ignore it. Act on it. Somebody needs what you have. Okay, so it may be a foolish act, but okay.

In June of 2010, I took the kids to Disney. It was a scary event for me. It was the first time I had gone anywhere without any other adults. Yet, it turned into an amazing time for me. I was able to get beyond my thoughts, relax, and enjoy the trip. It was a great time for reflection, but strange blessings began to happen. The first was a conversation with "Blue Cross Blue Shield" representative about insurance I had purchased. Something happened with a renewal that lingered for almost a year when they billed me for $600, a clear mistake. As I was talking with the representative, she said she had just received an email saying that I wouldn't have to pay the $600 for not being correctly charged the previous year. I thought, *That was interesting.* Then I got a one-day-free pass to the park when I went to buy an extra day. Could that have been the result of me paying for a pop for a teenage girl from Latin America the previous day while in the park? She was having a problem understanding what the man selling the pop was saying. Kyle was sitting there in amazement, wondering why I was buying this lady a pop. Before I could say anything, a lady in front of us said, "He is paying it forward," which means that at some point maybe that little girl would do something nice for someone else.

One weekend, I found myself crying in the driveway thinking about my godparents, Simpson and Manietta. I'd been trying to find a church to go to for a while, something different from the Episcopal Church I had been attending, one that was not rigid in formality. Sunday, I went to Woodside, a non-denominational church in Troy, Michigan. My first visit felt like I was home.

I still have my days when I fall down and fail at trying to be better, but I have learned to quickly recover. Just the other day, I was waiting for a friend, sitting in my car. He was late, and I started to get frustrated. Something in my head reminded me of what I tell myself every day. It's not always about me. I hadn't got the words out, and he called saying he was at the corner. Joel Osteen calls them tests. I think I passed that day.

The most incredible thing happened yesterday. A friend called and she was completely depressed with life. She complained about how she is always trying to be nice to everyone. I had suggested to her to keep on giving because it was part of her personality. Little did I know she was getting upset with me. She thought I was saying she was unworthy and didn't do enough for others. I decided to end the call and not let her ruin my day. I deleted her number and had decided not to ever call again. Then I realized I was just thinking about me and not trying to help another or show compassion. Funny thing, I deleted her number from my contacts, but she had called me, and the incoming number was still there. I called back and just listened.

She was talking about committing suicide. One of the things I had prayed about was the ability and skills to do bigger things for others. Little did I know it would be this! I talked to her for about an hour and convinced her that she needed counseling. I didn't know that the counseling I went through after being in a shooting would ever come up again. I was able to walk her through the process and explain how it could help. I even called the hospital and got her the number. She sent me an email last night, thanking me for possibly saving her life. She felt so relieved to have made the call to the hospital and for me sharing my experience. So, here is the interesting part. I had just left the gym and read a chapter that talked about being in the correct place at the correct time, that where I am today is where I'm supposed to be. Rather, it was a place for me to be to help another.

That night when everything returned to normal, I said, "Thank you, Ms. K." If she had not tired of my nonverbal commitment and lack of appreciation for all that she gave my sorry soul at the time, I would probably never have gone down this road or started this spiritual journey. That day was the first time that my heart was still and quiet.

I've read a number of times that God has a plan for all of us, but we must be in the right place at the right time, sow seeds for the future, and live each day to the fullest. Had it not been for this event, I might still be doing the same old dumb stuff I had been doing.

Sow seeds for the future, and live each day to the fullest.

So, every day I repeat my digital and written notes aloud so that I never forget the important stuff like:

- Teaching Kyle about manhood, respect, and looking at people when he speaks to them.

- To always show respect.

- Be there for others.

- Remember the world does not revolve around me.

- Continue to encourage Marnier and Kyle even when it is not a comfortable thing.

I laugh when I get a random email or text about staying on the path I'm on from someone who didn't even know I was on one. Maybe they can see the change I feel inside. And no, I have not seen any ghosts or talked to any dead people. I may talk to myself, but it is most likely me trying to correct a habit I'm trying to break. SO DO NOT TRY TO HAVE ME COMMITTED. I'm fine. As I helped my friend get off her wrong track to possible death and now recovery, I needed to get off my old tracks, onto a different road, heading a different direction. And no, don't expect to see me on a curb waiving a Bible, but you may see me doing more community-type stuff, although I have no clue what that might be.

Love,

Ray

~*\~

PRAYER

Mental Illness

Father, I'm hurt, not understanding the "why." I understand issues of the past and the ever present demons in our lives, the problem of mental illnesses. I'm not understanding how to help or where to intervene. I pray You pull back those on the cusp of suicide. Guide them toward that which they need. Amen, Amen, and Amen.

> *"Trust in the Lord with all thine heart; and lean not unto thine own understanding. In all thy ways acknowledge him, and he shall direct thy paths"* (Proverbs. 3:5-6).

Gracious Walk

CHAPTER 5

When the Lord Stops You

Remember the muse I mentioned previously? Well, she was back in Michigan visiting again. After getting home from Disney, I had plans to go visit my friend up in Port Huron who was back from California for the weekend. But weird things kept happening. The Friday I had planned to drive up, I had to plan an emergency party for Kyle's 13th birthday which I had forgotten the previous day. I rushed out, got him a gift card, planned his party, and we all had a good time. The next day, Saturday, I planned to drive to Port Huron after my Aunt Deb arrived from Virginia. I had a quarter of a tank of gas and had planned to fill up my tank in the morning and drive that afternoon. Normally, I spent Saturday with Mom and the crew. We went to the movies, had pizza, and right about the time Deb arrived, I got sick to my stomach. I went home and said, "If I feel better later, I will drive up and visit my muse friend." Dang, I wish I could remember her name.

About an hour or so later, I felt better and started the drive, which should have taken twenty minutes. I ended up taking me forty minutes to get to the expressway. When I finally got onto the highway, about five minutes into the drive, I realized that I didn't have any cash, no wallet, and thirty-one miles to go before my tank would be empty. I turned around and headed home, knowing I lived less than thirty-one miles from my home and money. At some point on the drive back home, the gas meter flipped to zero, and I was still four miles from home. As crazy as this may be, I was able to get all the way home where I had a full gas can. So clearly, I was not meant to see what I thought was my muse. For whatever reason the Lord had determined, I didn't need to see her and the next day she returned to California. A coincidence maybe, although, I get the impression she came into my life to get me to start reading again and that was it.

ᔆᴧᕀᔆ

INSPIRATIONAL THOUGHT

The Curve Ahead

We are all on a road headed somewhere, yet we can only see so far. Yet there exists a bend ahead, and we have no clue what's around it. Thus, we have to place 100% of our trust in the Lord. Grab His hand and enjoy the walk without fear of the unknown.

> *"Have not I commanded thee? Be strong and of a good courage; be not afraid, neither be thou dismayed: for the Lord thy God is with thee whithersoever thou goest"* (Joshua. 1:9).

CHAPTER 6

A Cross in the Picture

One day when I took Marnier to the doctor I was still reading It's Your Time by Joel Osteen. I got to a chapter about the human "will." I was taken aback a little, since part of my daily prayer was for God to fulfill what was in my heart. You guessed it. At the time, Ms. K still held a big piece of my heart, whether it was right, wrong, or misguided. It was what it was. I learned many years later that God will not change another person's will. He has given every human being free will to choose which way he or she will go. No matter how hard we pray or how long we stand in faith, things don't always turn out as we hope.

I was saying a little prayer while looking out the window, thinking what a great day it was going to be, and realizing I can't pray my way back into the past. But a strange thing happened right after that. When I turned around, there was a picture hanging on the wall, a picture with a bunch of flowers and right in the middle was a cross. I stared for a second thinking it was part of the picture. I looked away, looked back, and it was still there. So, I turned around, looked out of the window, and then turned back. It was gone, but this time I could see the full reflection of the AT&T building across the street. Okay, that was fine, just weird.

~\|/~

INSPIRATIONAL THOUGHT

Know Where Your Salvation Is

Following Jesus doesn't always make you a zealot. It makes you just wise enough to know where your salvation and refuge resides. We may not all make it, but I hope and pray you see God's throne.

> *"The Lord liveth; and blessed be my rock; and let the God of my salvation be exalted"* (Psalms 18:46).

CHAPTER 7

Can I Be Vulnerable (For the Fellas)?

Can we be vulnerable? Can we be vulnerable and still be seen as men? Can we be vulnerable in front of our sons? Can we be vulnerable in front of our home boys? Can we been seen as vulnerable in front of our wives or girlfriends? Webster's Dictionary defines the word vulnerable as, *"capable of being physically or emotionally wounded."* For this discussion, let us focus on being emotionally wounded. The essence of being vulnerable requires allowing ourselves to be exposed, and potentially take an emotional beating. The majority of time I've seen men allow themselves to be vulnerable is during a funeral. During that week after a friend or a loved one passes on, we are allowed to cry and not be judged, but that's about it.

Recently, I allowed myself to be vulnerable. I took a step over a line that said, "Cross at your own risk." As I lifted my leg over the barrier, I fell through a hole, and landed on an emotional roller coaster. It was a ride with major drops, dips, and curves. All I could do was question if crossing the line was outside of the Lord's plan as that little inner voice was quiet. That voice which guides my steps was not being critical of me. Even at times, it seemed as if that voice, through other actions, was nudging me to step over the line. Clearly, I was right where I was supposed to be. I was in the right emotional spot for God to work on me. He went to work, and today I can be vulnerable. I understand the importance of doing so as a man. Let me just note, it was painful, at times awful, but in the end, completely worthwhile. I can now open up and share my feelings. I can cry when I need to and share what I'm feeling with others without the feeling of condemnation.

The Bible is filled with stories of men being exposed and vulnerable. Nonetheless, they prospered through faith, prayer, and hope. So, I give you a resounding "Yes" to all of my initial questions.

━ᐊᑉᐅ━

INSPIRATIONAL THOUGHT

I'm Not Perfect

I'm not perfect. I make mistakes. I get things wrong, but I'm never too proud to say, "I'm sorry and seek forgiveness." Lord God, please keep spinning your potter's wheel. Keep molding me to be more like your Son, Jesus Christ. For as your hands shape me, I will be better today than I was yesterday.

> *"And be ye kind one to another, tenderhearted, forgiving one another, even as God for Christ's sake hath forgiven you"* (Ephesians 4:32).

> *"Then came Peter to him, and said, Lord, how oft shall my brother sin against me, and I forgive him? till seven times? Jesus saith unto him, I say not unto thee, Until seven times: but, Until seventy times seven"* (Matthew 18:21-22).

Gracious Walk

CHAPTER 8

Be Steadfast in Faith and Keep Holding On

Ravi Zacharias wrote in his book, *Has Christianity Failed You,* "From the Christianity perspective, the only roadblock to this celebration of God and to life as he has made it to be lived is because we have turned our backs on God, we are spiritually bankrupt" (Zacharias, 68).

So, you've endured periods or years of disappointments, loneliness, grief, failed relationships, unemployment, and you are a super magnet for trouble. You have prayed and prayed without receiving the results you expected. Perhaps you need to ask yourself a couple of questions and be honest with your answers. Are you still doing the same stupid things? Are you running the streets with the wrong crew? Are you being a pain to others? Are you minding everyone else's business and creating havoc? Are the couch and TV your best friends? So you are thinking God didn't respond to your prayers quick enough or He didn't respond at all. Kirk Franklin said in his book *The Blueprint: A Plan for Living Above Life's Storms,* "There may have been times when you had some delays in your life. It wasn't God saying, 'No.' It was God saying, 'Not yet.' Maybe God answered not yet" (Franklin, 194). Could it be He is waiting on you to get to the right place?

You must hold steadfast. Don't stop believing. Keep trusting vehemently that He will not abandon you. I beseech you not to hold God responsible.

You must hold steadfast. Don't stop believing.

I've shared with you in my blogs over the years how much my life has changed. I've shared with you some of my personal losses and crises, but this passage I think we can all understand. The Word says, *"Yea doubtless, and I count all things but loss for the excellency of the knowledge of Christ Jesus my Lord: for whom I have suffered the loss of all things, and do count them but dung, that I may win Christ"* (Philippians. 3:8). People refer to our Lord as the God of restoration. I've had restoration and experienced things that would make you scream hallelujah, jump for joy, and cry like a baby. Trust me, I have done all of this and more in expressing praise. What He has done for me through the years is enough to make me raise my hands and sing in public, hug anyone nearby, and pray often with gratitude and reverence.

Let me tell you a little about the following folks and the benefits of keeping your faith:

- The economy was tightening the vice grips on

my friend Marshall Williams. But one Friday morning, we staked a claim in prayer for a job he'd interviewed for, and it was his that same afternoon ~ God had his hand on the release lever.

• Teresa Mathis was taking a cab to work because her daughter who is away at school needed a car. A girlfriend of hers heard what Teresa had done and offered her the spare Mercedes in her garage ~ God gave Teresa more than she had or wanted.

• Annie Teague asked God to reveal her purpose. He responded, "Your words will be heard, and they have been by over 160+ people." Those words I have written about in my blogs. The Bible passages she shared with me provided comfort and guidance to others.

"Again, the kingdom of heaven is like unto treasure hid in a field; the which when a man hath found, he hideth, and for joy thereof goeth and selleth all that he hath, and buyeth that field" (Matthew 13:44).

God has amazing plans for you. So, call your Nana, Granny, or Big Mama. Ask her for a Bible. It will be well-seasoned like a cast iron pan right out of the kitchen and flavored to taste. I learned to stick prayers in my Bible from Grandma Peeples, and it works. Never turn away from your faith and belief. What is the worst thing that could happen by keeping your faith in God? You'll get what you already got. The best thing that could happen is you will get what He has prepared for you! Follow those instinctive goodness principles, be a giver to others, and reap the benefits of compassion.

Speaking of Bibles, God has an amazing way of getting someone's attention, either directly or indirectly. It was right before the holidays, and I began to think what about Christmas gifts for Lady P (aka another woman). As you've read, I think I have amazing taste in woman's clothing, so my focus was on shoes and dresses. See, I think when a man buys a woman a gift, it should be the entire ensemble. I do like a lovely lady in a dress, but I digress. In this particular case, everything I thought of, or was inspired by God to get, was red and black. I smashed open my piggy bank for a pair of red and black Louboutin shoes with a matching black dress. Notice, I said I had to break open my piggy bank. Those shoes are pricy, but she did say, "I like my heels." You can never go wrong getting her what she likes.

Then one night right around the beginning of November, I was praying in the closet upon my knees. I asked God, *"What do you want me to get her?"* and I distinctly heard a *"Bible."* I was just blown away. I went to bed that night just shaking my head in amazement. The next morning at the crack of dawn I was up and online searching for a Bible to order. I initially thought I would order from the same company Annie had purchased my Bible from (which had my name inscribed on it). But I could not find any ordering reference, so off to google.com I went. I found an online Bible store with countless Bibles and knew a New King James Version (NKJV) would be best. But which one to should I choose?

As I scrolled through the list of available Bibles, I saw the name Jenny, which is the same name as Lady P's daughter. Why was I not surprised that it was also a woman teaching Bible? I ordered it and had her name embossed on the cover. I received the Bible about a week later. It sat in my closet for weeks until one night, about a week before Thanksgiving, while again on my knees I heard, "Send it." I had it wrapped and then shipped. We may never understand how the Lord works, but we can know that He is indeed working all the time.

⁓⁄⁓

INSPIRATIONAL THOUGHT

Share the Word in Public

It is amazing how reading the Word of God in public will stop people dead in their tracks and dialogue begins. People want to know Him.

> *"This book of the law shall not depart out of thy mouth; but thou shalt meditate therein day and night, that thou mayest observe to do according to all that is written therein: for then thou shalt make thy way prosperous, and then thou shalt have good success"* (Joshua 1:8).

CHAPTER 9

Had My Dad Told Me, Just Maybe

> *"And not only that, but we also glory in tribulations, knowing that tribulation produces perseverance; and perseverance, character; and character, hope"* (Romans 5:3-4 NKJV).

The above verse had been on my mind for weeks after reading the book, *Dare to Be a Man: The Truth Every Man Must Know … and Every Woman Needs to Know about Him,* by David Evans. There was something about the verse that I hadn't been able to shake. The more I thought about it, the more I reread it and the clearer my understanding became concerning its meaning. It was a puzzle piece I needed to incorporate into my learning from the book I just finished, *For Men Only – A Straightforward Guide to the Inner Lives of Women,* by Shaunti Feldhahn. Don't let the title distill your thoughts on why I was reading it. Let me state on the record, it is my intent to improve every part of my life and character. So, let us be honest here, relationships are very big parts of our lives. We need to be better as the failure rate of relationships is astronomical, or at least that's how they appear from the outside looking in, knowing my own failure rates.

I don't ever remember a book that caused either an "ah-ha" moment, or memory flashes of missed opportunities for having built a stronger relationship in every single chapter. You know those times when I wished my dad had told me what to expect, how to respond, and how to be there for my girlfriend or wife. If I have to blame someone for my relationship failures, why not blame my dad. It is his fault. Okay, it wasn't, but that surely sounded good. I shifted the blame.

Allow me to share my level of manly ignorance over the years:

- She tells me she failed her nursing exam. My response, *"Don't worry about it. Just take it again."* – This was my missed opportunity to share in her sadness, not to offer advice on what she already knew she could and would do.

- She tells me her ex-boyfriend from Chicago keeps reaching out to her through Facebook and emailing her invitations to come to Chicago, Illinois. My response, *"Maybe you should go see him."* I missed my opportunity to be honest and tell her what I really thought and wanted. I was hurt by the attention she gave him. I wanted her to un-friend him. Clearly, he didn't respect our relationship, and

I thought she was actually considering his invitations.

- She tells me we don't spend enough time together, and she needs more of my attention than just on weekends and holidays. My response, *"Okay, I guess this is good-bye."* I missed my opportunity to have established ongoing date nights with a woman I loved unconditionally.

- She brings up past issues and hurts over and over. My response, *"Just forget about it. Let it go. That happened before me. You promised never to bring it up again."* This was a missed opportunity to understand her hurts and deepest thoughts.

WHAT MY DAD SHOULD HAVE TOLD ME

"Son, yes you love your mom, but you don't have enough time in your week to be there for both your mom and lady, no matter how hard you try to please both. You can love a woman and not give her what she needs, and she will leave, but your mom isn't going anywhere. There are going to be times that a woman will bring up an issue you thought was resolved. Don't just dismiss it, and tell her to forget it, or it's in the past. She may not be able to just forget it and may not be able to tell you why the issue is back. She's probably not attacking you."

I'm not a psychologist, but dig this, women have a lot of things on their minds all the time, and we men will never understand. It is possible something triggered an old issue or hurt, and she's trying to deal with it. Give her your undivided attention, listen to her concerns, and try to help her work through it. Stand with her. She has to always feel and know you love her. Let me quote some Scripture,

Give her your undivided attention, listen to her concerns.

"*Love is patient, love is kind. It does not envy, it does not boast, it is not proud. It does not dishonor others, it is not self-seeking, it is not easily angered, it keeps no record of wrongs. Love does not delight in evil but rejoices with the truth. It always protects, always trusts, always hopes, always perseveres*" (1 Corinthians 13:4-7 NIV).

So, let me tie this all together. The full passage containing the verse I started out with says, "*Therefore, having been justified by faith, we have peace with God through our Lord Jesus Christ, through whom also we have access by faith into this grace in which we stand, and rejoice in hope of the glory of God. And not only that, but we also glory in tribulations, knowing that tribulation produces perseverance; and perseverance, character; and character, hope*" (Romans 5:1-4).

Call it divine intervention, but the above scripture was presented to me in advance of the readings to help me get through the book's teachings. My "ah-ha" moments reminded me of my missed opportunities for building closeness, even sadness from failed relationships and tribulations. Yet, today even though I am enlightened, I still make mistakes. I am saddened that my enlightenment came so late in my life, but not so late that I couldn't change and teach my son. I had my son read one of the chapters in Shaunti Feldhahn's book as a learning opportunity. He was really surprised by the complexity of a woman's mind. Don't get me wrong, I still miss opportunities for closeness, but I'm much better at it today than yesterday. Today, I would rather apologize ten times, instead of never apologizing once. I never want to hurt or miss an opportunity for closeness with my special person.

My son will be smarter and more knowledgeable than me. Some godly woman will get an emotionally attuned man by the time he starts dating. I hope he gets a chance to be with one love for sixty years of happily married bliss.

～╲╷╱～

INSPIRATIONAL THOUGHT

Don't Be Afraid to Ask Your Father

I was like a little boy with my hands in my pockets, kicking stones and walking next to my Father, having a desire, but not asking for His help. I finally opened my mouth, asked, and immediately heard, "I've been waiting for you to ask." Now I'll wait and watch the heavens move on my behalf – Glory to God.

> *"Ask, and it shall be given you; seek, and ye shall find; knock, and it shall be opened unto you: For every one that asketh receiveth; and he that seeketh findeth; and to him that knocketh it shall be opened. Or what man is there of you, whom if his son ask bread, will he give him a stone? Or if he ask a fish, will he give him a serpent? If ye then, being evil, know how to give good gifts unto your children, how much more shall your Father which is in heaven give good things to them that ask him?"* (Matthew 7:7-11)

CHAPTER 10

Cultural Acceptance

As I travel the journey of life and share it with you, I continue to be amazed at the things and people that cross my path. So often through the years, I have heard people (ok.... Caucasians) speak of their cultural diversity, specifically, their cultural make-up for instance. They say, "I'm part German and Irish" or "I'm 10% Italian, 30% Dutch, and Canadian." From the black perspective, not speaking for all, we tend to see them as just being "Caucasian," as I tend to believe we are perceived as "just black" by them.

Recently, I had the pleasure of meeting a lady whom I was aware was part Asian, but her overall appearance looked 100% Latino. We had an interesting conversation about trying different things, like food for instance. Being ultra conservative about what I eat, I responded accordingly that, "I don't experiment." Not until later did I learn she was of Vietnamese heritage and descent. Thus, I understood what she was asking me. Yes, I felt a little hoodwinked, but it was actually to my naive benefit. I wouldn't have given a second thought to offering her collard greens, black-eyed peas, and cornbread, but I closed my mind to what foods were of her traditions.

This day, I invite you to open your eyes to someone else's culture. Step outside your comfort box, as I've asked her to share some of her cooking to get me out of my box. If I'm lucky, I'll learn a thing or two and will share some traditional cuisine from the Vietnamese region with you.

～ﾚﾟ

INSPIRATIONAL THOUGHT

A Helping Hand

My foot was stuck in the past and you pulled me out and pushed me forward. I fell face first into the mud and you handed me a towel. I kept pulling on a closed door and you told me, "It is locked. Let it go!" You taught me patience and forgiveness and surrounded me with godly people. Thank you Lord.

> *"Though he fall, he shall not be utterly cast down: for the LORD upholdeth him with his hand"* (Psalms 37:24).

CHAPTER 11

This Mercy Thing Is Confusing

I once sent a text message out about putting on your godly armor. If you remember, I asked you to, *"Put on the whole armour of God, that ye may be able to stand against the wiles of the devil. For we wrestle not against flesh and blood, but against principalities, against powers, against the rulers of the darkness of this world, against spiritual wickedness in high places. Wherefore take unto you the whole armour of God, that ye may be able to withstand in the evil day, and having done all, to stand. Stand therefore, having your loins girt about with truth, and having on the breastplate of righteousness; And your feet shod with the preparation of the gospel of peace; above all, taking the shield of faith, wherewith ye shall be able to quench all the fiery darts of the wicked. And take the helmet of salvation, and the sword of the Spirit, which is the word of God: Praying always with all prayer and supplication in the Spirit, and watching thereunto with all perseverance and supplication for all saints"* (Ephesians. 6:11-18).

You can put that Vera Wang dress or Hugo Boss back in the closet. Armor is what you need. I pray you are wearing it every day. It will never wear out, never get dirty. It will always shine brightly and can be worn 24/7.

One day I was perplexed. I had two people within an hour's span tell me, *"I can't forgive,"* for past acts of betrayals and treachery. Yet, for months I have seen them both show acts of mercy toward each other, though they both proclaimed having been wronged by the other. In my head, I was initially thinking that if people show mercy, are they not also forgiving? So, I had a bit of confusion. How can you not forgive, but show mercy? So off to the Bible I went, and I remembered this scripture from a sermon I once heard, *"For he shall have judgment without mercy, that hath shewed no mercy; and mercy rejoiceth against judgment"* (James 2:13). Thus, they may not yet be able to forgive, but the two friends were showing mercy above all else. Maybe it was just an accidental occurrence, but how cool were their actions toward each other. I am praying that they will have grace to take that challenging step of forgiveness, too. It's really important. Jesus taught if we can't forgive, then we can't be forgiven. That makes it serious.

> *Jesus taught if we can't forgive, then we can't be forgiven.*

Webster's Dictionary defines mercy as *"a blessing that is an act of divine favor or compassion"*. Stubbornness and my inability to forgive or show mercy has cost me dearly through the years, but each day I'm trying to be wiser. As my mother used to say, *"I had to learn the hard way.*" Maybe there is someone in your life that just needs mercy and forgiveness for some past unintentional or intentional act. Give it to them. Why don't you just grab them and give them a BIG hug. Join me in showing compassion and mercy every chance you get.

⁓

INSPIRATIONAL THOUGHT

Unashamed Blessings

It is God's sovereign power and wisdom on how He deals with our sins and blesses our lives. Work to be obedient, trusting, and faith filled. Be humble, but don't be ashamed of the blessing He bestows upon you.

> *"Give, and it shall be given unto you; good measure, pressed down, and shaken together, and running over, shall men give into your bosom. For with the same measure that ye mete withal it shall be measured to you again"* (Luke 6:38).

Gracious Walk

CHAPTER 12

Just Grab a Seat and Peddle

There was a time I felt as if I was getting out of sync with God and interfering in His plan. My focus was on everything other than Him and my allowance to let Him guide my steps. I was leaning on my own devices and doing just dumb stuff which I'm almost positively sure I thought was right. One morning around 2:00 am I just wasn't feeling right. I was experiencing an uneasy feeling. Can you remember a time when you were trying to talk to someone and that person turned his or her back? That individual acted as if he or she was not listening, yet you knew the opposite was true. These were the thoughts that would cross my mind as I prayed—as if the Lord was not listening, although deep down inside I knew that was not true. Then one morning, I thought I'd figured it out and off to the prayer closet I went. So, during my morning prayer I said aloud, *"I'm sorry, and I will get out of the way and let You (God) get back to guiding my life and steps."* That lack of godly presence lingered.

So, I went to the Waffle House and started only reading scriptures about obeying. I eventually read a scripture from Deuteronomy, *"This day the Lord thy God hath commanded thee to do these statutes and judgments: thou shalt therefore keep and do them with all thine heart, and with all thy soul. Thou hast avouched the Lord this day to be thy God, and to walk in his ways, and to keep his statutes, and his commandments, and his judgments, and to hearken unto his voice: And the Lord hath avouched thee this day to be his peculiar people, as he hath promised thee, and that thou shouldest keep all his commandments; And to make thee high above all nations which he hath made, in praise, and in name, and in honour; and that thou mayest be an holy people unto the Lord thy God, as he hath spoken"* (Deuteronomy 26:17-19).

I read it about three times over and over before one of the waitresses asked me for a scripture to get her through the day. So, I read that same scripture out loud to her (a first). Then another waitress walked up and asked if I was a pastor. She'd seen me reading the Bible there on a few mornings. I replied, "No." She began telling me how she believed in God. She told me how she prayed for His help and how He's blessed her. She even talked about some personal struggles. I held her hand, and we both started crying. I reminded her of the goodness of God and to remain faithful. I told her to keep praying and believing. We then prayed together, and the tears from my eyes just started flowing like a river. I had to run into the men's bathroom to regroup.

After leaving, I cried uncontrollably for another

fifteen minutes in my car. It felt like I was forgiven, used as His instrument to share the Gospel. Twelve hours later that day, I was still shaking from the morning and emotionally a spiritual wreck. I was still crying. There is nothing wrong with that. If someone had asked me why I was crying, I couldn't have explained it. So, here is the key. If you ask God for assistance and help, get out of the way and let Him work. Trust and obey. Grab a seat on the back of the tandem bike and just peddle. Keep peddling and let the Lord control the bike's direction and prepare for an exciting journey. It may not be down the road you want or desire, but trust me, it will be better than anything you could plan on your own.

~\l/~

INSPIRATIONAL THOUGHT
Humble Yourself

Our Lord is awesome. Just give Him a try! Humble yourself to His will and direction. Store up heavenly treasures, not earthly.

> *"Lay not up for yourselves treasures upon earth, where moth and rust doth corrupt, and where thieves break through and steal: But lay up for yourselves treasures in heaven, where neither moth nor rust doth corrupt, and where thieves do not break through nor steal: For where your treasure is, there will your heart be also"* (Matthew 6:19-21).

CHAPTER 13

Let Me Close My Mouth

> *"Enter through the narrow gate. For wide is the gate and broad is the road that leads to destruction, and many enter through it. But small is the gate and narrow the road that leads to life, and only a few find it"*
> (Matthew 7:13-14 NIV).

Some days can truly be whirlwind events, some positive and some just down right awful. I really try to walk the narrow path of the righteous, as they call it, not just in my personal behavior and thoughts, but how I treat other people, regardless of how my personal day is going. Yes, it can be a struggle not to just let a ferocious tongue loose and accompany it with rolling eyeballs and lots of indignation. Just give it as I've received it. I try hard to stay on that narrow path of righteous living as a Christian with a God-fearing lifestyle, essentially trying to treat others right, to help others, and to inspire others by controlling my tongue. The latter got away from me recently and my tongue clearly didn't know when to stop.

The Scripture says, *"Death and life are in the power of the tongue: and they that love it shall eat the fruit thereof"* (Proverbs 18:21). So instead of walking uprightly on the path, I fell and really scratched up both knees and hands. While down on all fours like an animal, I felt embarrassed and ashamed, because I was letting a lot of people down. I kept thinking *"How can I try to inspire you when my actions took me off the path?"* I finally told my failure to a couple people and one reminded me that I'm human. I will fail at times. There is no need to be ashamed. The other reminded me how she would never judge me because of a failure.

There is also pain and love in the other ways we communicate today, either through emails, text messages or social media. We all need to be conscious that through these different channels of communication our written word can be as fiery as an out of control tongue. I grew up in a household where folks would say, "Fine" or "Okay," and it wasn't with the intention of being cordial. It was purely disingenuous and an abrupt way of saying, "I am done with this conversation." Even in my later years, I still find myself using "Okay" in text messages. One day, my friend, Lady P, brought it to my attention and called me out about the context. It was like a sharp blade cutting to the marrow in my bones. On that day, she said, *"You just replied okay, and you were planning to let me leave town without resolving our issue."* Blessings to her for bridging that gap before she left town. It brought us peace, and eventually I received some nice pictures of her from Washington D.C. Since that day, I now try to never use the words "Okay" or "Fine," which may sound extreme, but I remember how it was used in my family.

The Bible mentions having wise counsel. *"The way of a fool is right in his own eyes: but he [or she] that hearkeneth unto counsel is wise"* (Proverbs 12:15). So, keep yourself surrounded with people who can speak the Word of God into your life. Keep yourself surrounded with people who will hold you accountable for your behavior. Seek good counsel in your lives as I have. I thank those who offered me a hand and helped me off the ground. My knees are bloody and will heal, but I'm up and walking forward again.

> *Keep yourself surrounded with people who can speak the Word of God into your life.*

The Word of God also says, *"The LORD your God in your midst, the Mighty One, will save; He will rejoice over you with gladness, He will quiet you with His love, He will rejoice over you with singing."* (Zephaniah 3:17 NKJV). Isn't it nice to know that even in our failures, the Lord will be right there holding us up, giving us a helping hand.

~\/~

PRAYER

Hear Our Prayers

Father, I ask that You hear the heart prayers of those who seek You. May You be glorified in all that we do this day!

> *"Be careful for nothing; but in every thing by prayer and supplication with thanksgiving let your requests be made known unto God"* (Philippians 4:6).

CHAPTE 14

Are You Listening for the Voice of God?

Today was one of those enlightening moments. I was having my monthly manly facial. Yes, I indeed said, "monthly facials." It can be a real struggle looking this handsome. Okay, so yes, I do make myself laugh at times, but in all honesty, men, as do women, need to take care of themselves. A little pampering is not really that unmanly. One day I'll have to tell you about my manicure and pedicure sessions.

On a monthly basis I get a facial, but I see it as just quiet time to pray and spend time in the presence of the Lord. My facial time has always been a great opportunity to really focus on the Lord. As I lay there, I experience all types of thoughts on corrections needed in my life, the needs of others, and time to seek wisdom and guidance. Also, when I'm in the presence of the Lord, I hear about ideas and things to share with you. At the end of one session, I heard His small voice speak, "Pray and obey." That was it! Just "pray and obey." As we both know, being obedient can be challenging at times. I think part of the problem is discernment. Are we hearing the voice of God or just what our minds are telling us to do? Are we hearing what we want to hear so that we can do what we really want to do?

I struggle with this from time to time, as do many. The key is testing what you hear against the Word of God. By this I mean, is what you believe you hear aligned with, or against the Word of God (aka Bible = Basic Instructions Before Leaving Earth). This will be a hard example, but it makes the point clear. You are not going to hear the Lord tell you it is okay to date another person's spouse. As they say in the hood, "It ain't going to happen." Typically, when I hear the Lord speak, it is not this long, drawn-out dialog. It is straight to the point in the most subtle manner. If you want to hear from the Lord, you need to have a personal relationship with Him, just you and Him.

So this day, I pray your ears and heart are circumcised so that you will not just hear, but listen when the Lord speaks to you. He is always speaking through His Word, but to hear Him, you need to study it.

‑‑‑‑

PRAYER

Noisy World

The noise and chaos of this world can be deafening. Turn it off if only for a short time every day. Find yourself a low-key, spirit-lifting, Gospel song and quiet your soul. Then go to God in prayer. Enjoy His presence and listen for His quiet voice giving direction. You'll find peace, guidance, and comfort. Peace we all need in our lives.

Father, I pray for all those whose lives and minds are cluttered with worldly noise. I pray You help them see Your guiding light. In Jesus' mighty name, Amen, Amen, and Amen.

> *"God is our refuge and strength, a very present help in trouble"* (Psalm 46:1).

CHAPTER 15

Break Every Chain That Holds You

O MG, I've been directly and indirectly spiritualized through two different godly interventions this day. Have you ever felt a sermon that was about you or directed toward you. I've had a few and experienced it with others, but I guess I was due AGAIN today.

I've been dealing with some personal issues and to paraphrase Joyce Meyer, "The enemy starts working on us the moment we awake." Sadly, an underworld spirit had my attention early, and by 6:00 am I was three pages into my written wrath doctrine. Having put my pen down, I laid on the couch, awaiting peace and inner satisfaction. Then I heard that inner voice tell me to get the doctrine and destroy it. What I had done was not my path to walk. I obeyed.

Fast forward to church and the last couple of weeks the sermon had been on *Why Do the Righteous Suffer?* It was kind of interesting until the sermon felt like it was about me. I sensed that the sermon was about a terrible habit I had that had a destructive effect on others around me. The weird part was

I had just finished praying, asking for help. I made God a promise to never let it be a part of my life again. Halfway through the sermon, it felt like God had accepted my promise. Through pastor, I was being taught about the destructive nature of "shutting down." Father then gave me clear instructions through Pastor Carl how to behave going forward. As I sat there with a trembling body and mind, in awe, I said aloud, "I hear You, Father, and will obey!"

God wasn't done. He wanted to make sure I got it. Pastor Carl read 1 Corinthians 12:26 – *"If one part suffers, all parts suffer with it, and if one part is honored, all parts are glad."* Now that's how you get an immediate answer. Amen to the power of prayer.

◦

INSPIRATIONAL THOUGHT

Pray as Long as You Need or He Requires

I opened my mouth to pray for a couple things on my mind and the list explodes exponentially as the Holy Spirit guides.

> *"Rejoice evermore. Pray without ceasing. In every thing give thanks: for this is the will of God in Christ Jesus concerning you"*
> (1 Thessalonians 5:16-18).

CHAPTER 16

God Doesn't Hate You or Me

L et me just get to it. How does anyone respond to the comment A friend at work recently blurted out, "God hates me" How does anyone respond to a comment like that?? This conclusion was based on the fact that she was single. My heart just sunk as there was nothing I could say other than, "Keep your faith and believe that things will change." Yet mentally I was blown away by her comment of being hated, especially when God says, *"For I know the thoughts that I think toward you, saith the Lord, thoughts of peace, and not of evil, to give you an expected end"* (Jeremiah 29:11). Maybe it is just me, but that doesn't sound like He hates her, you, or me. I'm encouraged by that scripture and the promises it contains.

Who in the world has never been single or desired to be in a relationship? I know this is hard to believe, but I've been single on more occasions than I'd like to count, even on probably the worst day of the year, that dreaded Valentine's Day, wishing I had someone to share it with. Even so, I have never known any of my friends or family reaching a point of feeling God hated them because they were single. If one of them ever felt that way, it was never verbally expressed. It's such a hard concept to think God would hate people because they don't have a man or woman in their lives.

Let me share a story about something I recently saw. I was sitting at Starbucks, working one Friday morning. A lady walks in, orders food and a drink. She sits across from me and I think, *She's a nice-looking woman, nowhere near as lovely as Lady P, but nice.* Then she starts to eat with her mouth open. I think, *That is interesting,* and go back to minding my own business. A little while later a young man walks in. Orders food and drink. As he is standing at the counter waiting on his food, I see him look at that same lady, except he had a weird expression and was just staring. I thought, *That is kind of creepy.* He gets his order and walks over to her. She stands up and they kiss. I thought, *Oh my, I didn't see that one coming.* He sits down and begins to eat his food with his mouth open. I laughed and thought, *Yep, there is someone for everyone,* and returned to minding my own business.

So, with thoughts of you, I hope and pray that you never let the unseen evil of this world mislead your mind. I beseech you to keep your faith and belief during the hardest of times. We will all have times of struggles; that's just

Keep your faith and belief during the hardest of times.

life. Today, I'm dealing with a personal situation that has left me numb and speechless. I have no clue how to resolve it, so I put on my spiritual armor as I should and press forward. I continue to pray, hope, and seek spiritual wisdom, believing the best is yet to come.

━━

PRAYER

Bullied

Thank you, Lord. You took a "bullied" child who probably should be hate-filled and gave him a humbled and open heart, and a gentleness that attracts folks who need to vent and get rid of their burdens. He stills needs more work, but he thanks You greatly. He thanks You for the godly folks he's surrounded by.

> *"For by grace are ye saved through faith; and that not of yourselves: it is the gift of God"* (Ephesians 2:8).

CHAPTER 17

Are We Detrimental in Our Relationships Just Being Ourselves?

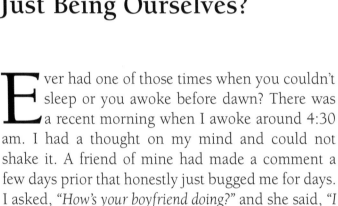

E ver had one of those times when you couldn't sleep or you awoke before dawn? There was a recent morning when I awoke around 4:30 am. I had a thought on my mind and could not shake it. A friend of mine had made a comment a few days prior that honestly just bugged me for days. I asked, *"How's your boyfriend doing?"* and she said, *"I can screw up a relationship all on my own without any help."* Thus, they aren't together anymore. Wow!

The following Sunday the sermon was, as you can guess, on relationships. An associate pastor was teaching on that subject and mentioned that relationships are not 50/50. Relationships are 100/100 which means that 100% of your focus has to be on ensuring the happiness of your partner. Only then can you truly eliminate issues. I was thinking during service, *50/50 seems so much better.* In my head I was thinking, *I give and she takes. Sounds perfect.* The associate pastor then said and I paraphrase, *"50/50 means that you are really just thinking about your own needs."* Dang it, I hate it when someone reads my mind during service. Please get out of my head. I'm having a personal conversation with myself.

So, are we detrimental to relationships? When your significant other did something special for you, did you embrace it wholeheartedly? This morning, did you just walk out the house screaming a non-heartfelt "Goodbye? Did you say "Goodbye" at all? Do the people you consider special in your life know it? Did you speak something positive into their lives to motivate them today and let them know they are loved?

Allow me to share this scripture with you, *"Love must be sincere. Hate what is evil; cling to what is good. Be devoted to one another in love. Honor one another above yourselves. Never be lacking in zeal, but keep your spiritual fervor, serving the Lord. Be joyful in hope, patient in affliction, faithful in prayer. Share with the Lord's people who are in need. Practice hospitality. Bless those who persecute you; bless and do not curse. Rejoice with those who rejoice; mourn with those who mourn. Live in harmony with one another. Do not be proud, but be willing to associate with people of low position. Do not be conceited"* (Romans 12:9-16 NIV).

So, if that bit of Scripture was on your mind this morning when you awoke and engaged your wife and children, do you think your morning and this day might be different? I'm talking about you and your actions, not what the other person did or didn't do. You might have what potentially 10 million scary subscribers on match.com desire and without the fifty dollar a month charge. So, I leave you with this question, are you detrimental in your relationship or beneficial? Some of you right now will do something to answer me with an astounding, "NO, NOT ANYMORE!" Others will respond by a loving action you're about to do right now or in the future.

⌐ᴵ⌐

PRAYER

I Need Your Help

Thank You Lord for all that You do for me. Father, I ask that You reveal to me the things I need to change that hinder my relationship with my wife and children. Father I know that I'm not perfect and I pray for forgiveness of my failures, guidance to improve, and instruction to build strong bonds with all those under my care. Lord, I know I can't do this without You and I don't even want to try unless You help me. In Jesus' name I pray. Amen, Amen and Amen.

CHAPTER 18

The Lord Can Change You; I'm Proof

During a three day fast, I was having all kinds of thoughts, images, and amazing dreams. I initially awoke that morning with some confused thoughts, thoughts on things I just didn't understand and my mind answering them all incorrectly. As I opened my eyes, on my wall appeared an image of a cross. It literally was moving back and forth between two walls. I stared in amazement as the sight reminded me of God's presence. Go figure, the image was due to men working on the golf course behind my home and their lights reflecting through my window. Funny how God will use anything at His disposal to remind us of His presence.

I believe the key is seeking and letting Jesus into your life. Once you do that, anything is possible. As I prayed that morning, I thanked God for moving me from 'over there' to right where I needed to be—so He could reveal what I needed to work on. That day it was revealed that I needed to work

The key is seeking and letting Jesus into your life.

on the issues within my own home, my own inner circle. In other words, the needs of others outside of my family shined brightly, but I was missing the needs of those closest to me. The need to get my own spiritual house in order was at the top of my priority list. I needed to do for my own family what I was doing for others outside of my house.

Humbling ourselves and submitting to God will open our eyes. But to be enlightened can be scary. To let Him fix us can be painful if we fight it, but the resulting change has the most dynamic effect. That year, I saw God's mercy sober a man cold turkey overnight after thirty years of drinking. I've seen an atheist come to Christ. I watched a sister hug her brother (me) for the first time in fifty years. I thank Him and praise Him for the amazing change and eye-opening experiences in my life.

‑‑‑

INSPIRATIONAL

Tap into God's Strength

Tap into God's strength, His power, His joy. Do not align yourself with the misery, disheartenment, or grief of the one that works against our Lord.

> *"Every word of God is pure: he is a shield unto them that put their trust in him"*
> (Proverbs 30:5).

Gracious Walk

CHAPTER 19

Angry

Before Christ, I was a two headed coin. On one side of the coin I was a pleasant, humble, gentle, and kind man. On the other side, I was easily angered and filled with uncontrollable meanness—so uncontrolled, there was no regret, no conviction, and no remorse.

An intervention was required, and God needed to get my attention, but having a mind full of turmoil made hearing His voice impossible. We'll never understand His ways, but through two heartbreaks, things began to change. The first heartbreak resulted in days of indescribably painful thoughts and confusion. I was a wanderer searching for answers where no human understanding existed. Then on Good Friday many years ago, while blindly driving, I ended up in the parking lot of an Episcopal church. From that moment, life would never be the same again. That was the day the molding of my heart began and the Word of God became alive in me.

Years later the emotional turmoil still existed and was wreaking havoc within my Florida family. Once again, God needed to directly intervene. As I watched my family walk out the door and the tears flowed, I knew I needed help. God's grace and mercy guided me to an amazing counselor and a men's church group for support. Through counseling, I was able to fully understand where all the anger originated and how it had hindered my personal life. This was a truly-sad, passed-down, generational anger trait. Today, God's mighty hand and strength governs my behavior and thoughts. I'm aware of when I need to step back and settle my mind.

My father never taught me manhood or the actions thereof. My grandfather (aka Big Daddy) showed me how to be kind and giving, but manhood and its meaning was allusive. The visual of a "real man" was one that is financially stable, married, raising his kids, and loving his amazing wife whom he is building a future with. These were all the things I thought made me a man, but it never made me feel like one. Sad were the days I would hear any woman say, "This is what men do." Whenever a woman spoke those words, they were clueless to the crushing of my spirit, triggering an angry outburst. Yet she didn't know the pain it caused, as no man would ever tell a woman he didn't feel like a man. It is hard to describe the feeling as I gracefully aged year after year. Through the men's group, I learned that was what I was feeling and dealing with. Many in the group had faced the same challenges. In our wagon train circle, I heard their stories and shared mine. Glory to God, I wasn't alone and the man within me finally arose.

Today, I still have moments of not feeling like a man, but I recognize that I am a work in progress. I'm still flesh, with immature emotions, but with a different nature and a different way of responding. I'm deeply saddened for any pain I have caused. Yet, I thank God I am not the person I used to be. I see myself in the mirror and still ask, "Who are you?" and I answer the same way, "A child of the Most High God." Then I give God praise and thanks for never abandoning me and His continued blessings.

~\\/~

PRAYER

Our Trust in the Lord

Father, thank You for another day. Father, I offer up my praise and blessings. Father, I pray for my family and friends, those with life, relationship, loss, and job issues. Father, we seek Your strength. Father, help us feel Your presence and place 100% of our trust in You and only Your plan for our lives. Amen, Amen, and Amen.

> *"And he said unto me, My grace is sufficient for thee: for my strength is made perfect in weakness. Most gladly therefore will I rather glory in my infirmities, that the power of Christ may rest upon me"*
> (2 Corinthians 12:9).

CHAPTER 20

Saved by Grace

Some nights I should not even go to sleep. I should just stay awake because my body is determined to wake before the sun rises. One morning recently, I awoke. It was around 3:30 am. I literally needed to pinch my cheeks to get a little color and my blood flowing. Ok, maybe not too much color, as my skin is quite dark, but just a pinch to get the blood flowing. Those who know me, know I arise every morning fairly early. I think it must be a generational thing. My grandmother used to do the same thing. Every morning she was up before the sun arose. I guessed this habit carried throughout her life as she grew up on a farm. Every morning she would rise with Auntie Fanny to cook breakfast for the farm help on Great-granddaddy's farm in Augusta, Georgia. I spent a lot of time as a child with her, and I guess the early morning "rise and shine" thing stuck with me.

Thus, daily I'm up early to pray, walk with God, and have a conversation with Him during the quiet morning time before the days get started. As the Scripture says, *"I love them that love me; and those that seek me early shall find me*" (Proverbs 8:17). Yet, that morning I was awakened even earlier because of a comment someone said to me the previous night. Maybe you've experienced it, but there is an old saying, *"The last thing you think about at bedtime is the first thing you think about the next morning."* So, I had a conversation with a friend and shared with him upcoming events that I was happy about and looking forward to. His response was, "You're a sinner!" Whoa, where did that comment come from, even in joking? I immediately thought, *Who says that to someone without any kind of other preceding comment, context, or something to provide clarity?"* It is one of those comments that mentally takes you somewhere negative, then just drops you off, abandoned, and bewildered. Clearly, I was shocked and dismayed. The only thing I could think was, *"Well, that's encouraging. I just shared with you an upcoming event that I was thrilled about, and you just grabbed the rug from under me and laid me flat out on the ground."*

That night I remember just lying on the floor and staring at the ceiling, reliving that comment over and over in my head. The next morning that "sinner" comment was the very first thing that popped into my mind. As I laid there in bed praying, I started thinking of people who have been used greatly by God who were not perfect. I thought about Paul (Saul) who persecuted those who didn't follow the Jewish laws, who accepted Jesus as the Messiah, and what happened to him on the road to Damascus.

"Then Saul, still breathing threats and murder against the disciples of the Lord, went to the high priest and asked letters from him to the synagogues of Damascus, so that if he found any who were of the Way, whether men or women, he might bring them bound to Jerusalem. As he journeyed he came near Damascus, and suddenly a light shone around him from heaven. Then he fell to the ground, and heard a voice saying to him, 'Saul, Saul, why are you persecuting me?' And he said, 'Who are You, Lord?' Then the Lord said, 'I am Jesus, whom you are persecuting. It is hard for you to kick against the goads.' So he, trembling and astonished, said, 'Lord, what do you want me to do?' Then the Lord said to him, 'Arise and go into the city, and you will be told what you must do'" (Acts 9:1-6 NKJV).

As I laid there thinking, this one Romans scripture came to mind, "For all have sinned and fall short of the glory of God" (Romans 3:23 NKJV). That was my 'wow' moment, thus this boat that I'm in, this boat where I feel like I'm a sinner. I'm not in a boat by myself. It's a boat full of people floating on God's mercy and His grace. In this boat, I can look back and see the person who called me a sinner sitting over in a corner. I can look forward and see pastors who lead amazing churches. I can see other people who have amazing ministries in hospital visitations and food pantries. I can see people in this boat, people who have big hearts for the needs of others. They are natural givers of themselves for people in need. So, I'm thinking, "Hold up a minute. This boat is filled with other sinners, people who make mistakes and fall *short of His glory, but still are greatly used."* God is still using me; He's still using you. Let me repeat the key verse, "For all have sinned and fall short of the glory of God" (Romans 3:23). Shortly thereafter, I was feeling okay. Yes, I'm a sinner, but I'm not alone. There are a lot of people in this boat with me. Oh yes, I have repented and do all I can to live in the truth. Oh yes, the Bible calls me and the rest of God's people *"saints"* (1 Corinthians 1:3). But we still fall short at times. Yet, God will still use us, if we humble ourselves and are sincere in our commitment to Him.

> *God will still use us, if we humble ourselves.*

He can use you. He will use you. History has shown that people who made big mistakes, huge mistakes, can still be used by God—after they take the steps to get things right. So, when you get up in the morning and you're looking at that person in the mirror, say to yourself, "On my own, I'm a sinner but by His grace I'm saved. God can still use me even though I have failures in my past. He will use me because I honor Him. He still blesses my life, because I surrender to Him. He's still in control of my life. He is my life. I'm a child of the God."

∼∿∼

INSPIRATIONAL THOUGHT

Without God's Help, I Am Just a Sinner

On my own, without God's help, I'm a sinner, I'm sinful and I sin, but Lord, thank You that I'm not bound to my past or this life. You've given me a path to righteousness and forgiveness. Lord, I thank You for all you do, seen and unseen, for those around me who keep me in their prayers as do I for them. Thank You, Lord. *"For all have sinned, and come short of the glory of God; Being justified freely by his grace through the redemption that is in Christ Jesus"* (Romans 3:23-24).

.

CHAPTER 21

A Crazy "Dead People" Dream

I just awoke from the craziest dream. It was resurrection day. I was at the Woodlawn cemetery
in Detroit and I found myself standing with my
cousin Donnie and someone else. It appears the other person was from a wealthy family. It was his job
to release members of his family from their family
crypt. There was a padlock on the crypt and nobody
had a key. I reached down and pulled the padlock
right off this little box in front of the crypt and inside
were keys.

So, the man began opening the individual family
vaults to release people. When he opened one of the
caskets it was empty except for gold bars and other
jewelry. I asked, *"What did that person do, try to take all
their money and wealth with them?"* He said, "Yes." I remember saying to Donnie, *"It appears he went down."* I
assumed that meant to hell, but I didn't ask anything
else. The sun was shining, and it was a beautiful day
outside and as I looked around, I could see all these
other people rising from the graves.

My cousin Donnie and I started walking, and I

saw our old bodies begin to change into young men again. We both were amazed. We walked up to an elevator and went inside. The inside was really small; only a few people could fit. The door closed. It started going up and eventually stopped.

When the door opened, we walked out and my cousin and the other man turned left, but some lady at a desk called me forward. It was like a little office and she was sitting behind a desk as were three other women. She said, *"Belzar is looking forward to meeting you."* I didn't recognize the name, but I knew then something wasn't right. She motioned me to stand directly in front of her desk and behind me was a white sheet hanging from the ceiling. She said, *"I need to take your photo."* Clearly my cousin and the other person had gone to be with the Lord, but I was left behind.

As I stood there I said, *"When will I meet God?"* All three ladies jumped backward in their seats. They seemed afraid when I said God's name and kind of shook their heads against my question about God. Then I said His name again and again. They jumped again and again. That is when I knew something wasn't right. I started praying "the Lord's Prayer" out loud I started telling this woman about the goodness of God. There was this bright light arising behind me. The whole room lit up. As I began to walk away and head toward this comforting light, she asked, *"If I could, could I come visit?"* and I said, *"You would if you started to believe."* She said, *"I will,"* and I awoke.

This dream was just strange, and to this day I don't fully know the meaning.

─ᴧ⁄ᵉ─

PRAYER

Revelation of Life, Death, and Resurrection

Lord, as we think on the life, death, and resurrection of Jesus, I pray You reveal the intense and Spirit-filled relationship between these events. Help us, Lord. I ask, hope, and pray that You strengthen our spirits. *"But the Comforter, which is the Holy Ghost, whom the Father will send in my name, he shall teach you all things, and bring all things to your remembrance, whatsoever I have said unto you"* (John 14:26).

Gracious Walk

CHAPTER 22

The Lord
Is Working

You know there are some messages you cannot type in forty characters and too detailed to type as a Facebook post. I stand in awe of God's goodness, how He works, and the way things happen in a believer's life. There is a restaurant I like visiting in Orlando, Florida. I was there one night watching the baseball game. This older couple came in and immediately, I felt a connection to them. I don't know why, as I have never met or seen them before, but there was just something very special about them. They ended up sitting at a table next to me and shortly thereafter, three additional family members arrived and joined them. Then they were in need of an additional table, so I gave them one of mine as I was sitting at a four top and I was alone.

Feeling appreciative, he offered to buy me a drink and I gracefully declined. He continued to ask and I continue to declined. Finally, he said, "Can I buy you a water?" and we both laughed. We continued to talk, and he shared all kinds of very interesting stuff. He told me about the woman next to him, that she had been single for forty years and now they were together. Seeing them interact and talk was awesome. They appeared to have a radiant light just emanating from them.

He was retired military and both were also retired civil servants. We had this awesome dialogue going. I wondered which one had prayed to have that special person brought into their life. God ultimately provided for them. It got me to thinking the Scripture says, *"Be strong and of a good courage, fear not, nor be afraid of them: for the Lord thy God, he it is that doth go with thee; He will not fail thee, nor forsake thee"* (Deuteronomy 31:6). So being the person that I am, I dropped my head, said a little prayer for them, and eventually said good night and left.

The next morning, at the crack of dawn, around 4:30 am, I was awakened and was in prayer mode. My mind was on the two people from the previous night. There was something about the number forty that keep resonating in my mind; I thought about all the times forty appears in the Bible.

- Forty days and nights in which there was a flood on the earth and God's promise: "And I will establish my covenant with you, neither shall all flesh be cut off any more by the waters of a flood; neither shall there any more be a flood to destroy the earth" (Genesis 9:11).

- Forty years in which the Hebrews walked in the wilderness and God's promise: *"And I am come down to deliver them out of the hand of the*

> *Egyptians, and to bring them up out of that land unto a good land and a large, unto a land flowing with milk and honey; unto the place of the Canaanites, and the Hittites, and the Amorites, and the Perizzites, and the Hivites, and the Jebusites"* (Exodus 3:8).Again, He's promised to never leave us or forsake us.

- Forty days in which Moses was on the mountain top.

- Forty days in which Jesus was in the desert.

I know we all are praying for some things, waiting for some things, but this just reminds us that God is always working for us. He's always present. We can hold tight the scripture that says, *"For I know the thoughts that I think toward you, saith the Lord, thoughts of peace, and not of evil, to give you an expected end"* (Jeremiah 29:11). We can also hold onto this Word. *"And whatsoever ye shall ask in my name, that will I do, that the Father may be glorified in the Son. If ye shall ask any thing in my name, I will do it"* (John 14:13-14). So, hang in there, keep fighting, and keep praying for those things your heart desires.

Just hold on and know the Lord is working, but while you are holding on, don't forget to be a blessing, plant a seed into someone's life. Do things lovingly. Help those who are in need. Yes, there will always be someone in need, and I know we can't help everyone, but there are some people who help no one. Don't be that person. Plant a seed. Sow a seed and wait for the bounty. The Scripture says, *"But this I say, He which soweth sparingly shall reap also sparingly; and he which soweth bountifully shall reap also bountifully"* (2 Corinthians 9:6). Seed every chance you get.

Plant a seed. Sow a seed and wait for the bounty.

━⁖━

PRAYER

A Blessed Life

Lord, thank You for such an amazing and blessed life. You hear our prayers and answer. You put a roof over our heads, food in our fridge, and You've surrounded us with loving, Spirit-filled people. My legs feel weak, yet I'm still upright. We are so thankful for everything, and we praise Your holy name with every breath. Undeserving we are, yet we hold tight to Your written Word, *"Let your conversation be without covetousness; and be content with such things as ye have: for he hath said, I will never leave thee, nor forsake thee"* (Hebrews 13:5).

CHAPTER 23

Power of Prayer

There is something very powerful about the power of prayer. That is your time with the Lord Jesus. I really hope today you find some time just to find yourself a quiet place, get alone, get down on your knees, sit in a chair or lean against a wall, and just open your heart unto Him. Have a one–on–one personal time between you and Him. Share the things that are on your mind and the thoughts you have. Have a conversation with an open heart and do not try to hide anything. He knows all of your secrets even if you don't share them. Talk to Him. Ask questions, but be listening for His response and directions, because He will be talking back. And He will answer you. Prayer is powerful. It is just a relationship between you and Him.

━☀━

INSPIRATIONAL THOUGHT

Take a Moment to Be Still

In the morning, before you jump out of bed why don't you take a few minutes, lay there, say a little prayer and then just listen for His quiet voice. The Lord might have something to tell you. You might even feel a level of needed peace.

> *"Be still, and know that I am God: I will be exalted among the heathen, I will be exalted in the earth"* (Psalms 46:10).

CHAPTER 24

The Lord Takes Care of His Own

I want to share a quick little story with you that happened last night. I needed a couple of gift cards for a charity event that I was planning to attend later in the evening. I honestly just totally forgot about it all day. A couple hours before the event, I remembered the need. That evening I got dressed, jumped in the car, and thought I could make a quick stop somewhere to get the gifts cards before dinner. I said aloud, *"Lord, where can I stop?"* and He replied, *"Barnes and Noble."* I thought, *Perfect, it's on my way and in the same direction as the restaurant.* As I'm exiting, I began to think, *I don't really need to make that stop, I have a couple gift cards in my pocket that I carry as blessing gifts.* As I got closer to the restaurant, I feel that tug to just go to Barnes and Nobel and grab the cards. I went inside, got a couple of cards and headed to the counter. The cashier said, *"Oh, these cards have little gifts."* The cashier assembled the boxes and inserted the cards. I wrote the amounts on them and hand her money.

The cashier then said, *"You also will receive a third gift card for free."* I'm thinking, *What I am going to do* with a third gift card. *I don't really shop at Barnes No-ble. I order books online whenever I purchase one, but, I won't argue. I'll just accept it.* I thought to myself, *This card is going to be sitting in my wallet for who knows how long.* I got my change, grabbed the gift boxes with the cards inside and headed toward the door. I literally walked outside the building and off to the right, I see this lady wrapped in blankets sitting on the bench. Homeless, I assumed. She's was wrapped in blankets, just sitting there. I walked over to her, pulled that third gift card out of my pocket and hand-ed it her. I said, "Why don't you go inside, get a coffee and snack." She responded, *"Thank you,"* and I left. It immediately reminded me that the Lord takes care of his own; we just have to be obedient.

> *The Lord takes care of his own; we just have to be obedient.*

We only need to listen, keep our eyes open, and pay attention. The opportunity to serve will present itself. You just need to act. I've heard people say, *"The Holy Spirit is the voice of God, Jesus is the face of God, and we are his hands and feet."* I thought that was kind of awesome example of God taking care of His own.

‑‑\‑‑

INSPIRATIONAL THOUGHT

Tap into God's Strength

Tap into God's strength, His power, His joy, not the misery, disheartenment, or grief of the one that works against our Lord.

> *"The thief cometh not, but for to steal, and to kill, and to destroy: I am come that they might have life, and that they might have it more abundantly"* (John 10:10).

Bear Another's Burden

It may not feel like it, but when someone shares a burden, the strength of your back is helping lift it off of them.

> *"Though I am free and belong to no one, I have made myself a slave to everyone, to win as many as possible. To the Jews I became like a Jew, to win the Jews. To those under the law I became like one under the law (though I myself am not under the law), so as to win those under the law. To those not having the law I became like one not having the law (though I am not free from God's law but am under Christ's law), so as to win those not having the law. To the weak I became weak, to win the weak. I have become all things to all people so that by all possible means I might save some. I do all this for the sake of the gospel, that I may share in its blessings"*
> (1 Corinthians 9:19-23 NIV).

CHAPTER 25

A Personal Relationship with Jesus

I t was 3:30 am, and Charles Stanley was on TV. I caught a little bit of his sermon on patience. It kind of echoed in me as I prayed and then laid down again before getting up and heading to church. I pulled myself together a couple hours later, got dressed, and finished reading my daily devotional before heading out the door. The very last sentence in the daily devotional was a reference to the prayer that Jesus prayed before going to the cross, "Father, if thou be willing, remove this cup from me: nevertheless not my will, but thine, be done" (Luke 22:42).

That last sentence resonated with me in the car as I was driving. I began to think about my past relationships and past hurts, and I was reminded of God's goodness. Having a relationship with Him allows you to see things differently in your life. He heals relationships that may have failed because of your relationship with Him. He teaches and reveals those

Having a relationship with Him allows you to see things differently in your life.

things that could have been done better, so you can learn from your mistakes. He molds us in the form of Jesus. He restores broken hearts, teaches us how to love ourselves and others.

As my drive to church continued, I started thinking about Christianity—and what I want you to understand is Christianity is not this blown out religious thing. It's not heavy upon you. It is strictly just your personal relationship with the Lord Jesus Christ. It is not about going to church seven days a week or attending every event. It is just about your personal relationship with Him and then out of that relationship is all the other stuff that comes along with it. You might want to go to church, congregate, worship and share those moments on a Sunday, a Wednesday, or some other day of the week. You might even join a ministry group and out of this new path, you'll become His hands and feet, blessing others and serving in your community. Out of that relationship, He becomes your place of refuge to go when you are hurting or someone in your family is sick, your place of comfort, peace and spiritual renewal.

That place for life's instructions are all generated out of that personal relationship, the blessings, the grace, and the mercy upon your life. I'll be the first to tell you that being a Christian and following Jesus does not mean everything negative goes away, that there's no pain, no agony, or no unhappiness. That's the earthly stuff that happens in all our lives, but we have a place to go for comfort. We have a place to go where the Holy Spirit teaches us how to be better people. He teaches us how to walk through that the tough times, how to help someone else who is walking through a storm. I can't tell you the number of people that I know, and I've been humble enough to be a part of their lives, to walk with them through some tough things they were going through, folks I've had the opportunity to pray for and who prayed for me even when they were going through a struggle. That is the blessing, unity, and love that the Lord Jesus teaches us through the Word of God.

Religion and Christianity is not a fringe thing where you go on Easter, when you think you need to go buy a new suit or buy a new dress to make your best appearance. It is not a Christmas Eve thing either when people think, *I better go to church tonight because I want to celebrate the birth of Jesus. Or aNew Year's Eve thing, Because I don't want to miss out on the blessing of bringing in the New Year in a watch night service.* Okay, so you go one night but you do nothing else the rest of the year. That's just not how this thing works. It's an ongoing, three-hundred-sixty-five days a year with various activities filled with God's love. I'm not the best at it but I'm learning; I'm continually trying to learn. Hopefully I'm better today than I was yesterday, but it's an ongoing thing, and it's strictly out of my personal relationship with the Lord Jesus Christ. It is a relationship available to everyone.

～ヽノ～

INSPIRATIONAL THOUGHT

Blessing Chase Me

Blessings are chasing me down! I thank You, Lord, for each and every one of them.

> *"And all these blessings shall come on thee, and overtake thee, if thou shalt hearken unto the voice of the Lord thy God. Blessed shalt thou be in the city, and blessed shalt thou be in the field. Blessed shall be the fruit of thy body, and the fruit of thy ground, and the fruit of thy cattle, the increase of thy kine, and the flocks of thy sheep. Blessed shall be thy basket and thy store. Blessed shalt thou be when thou comest in, and blessed shalt thou be when thou goest out"* (Deuteronomy 28:2-6).

CHAPTER 26

Serving in Church

I can't think of anything more humbling than serving others. There is so much more to discipleship than what is happening on the platform every Sunday. Yes, we need ministers to teach and preach the Gospel, but I truly believe it is the hands and feet of others that connect it all together.

When believers take the time to serve in the church or their community, they not only benefit others, but there is an internal personal benefit also. We get to open up our lives by giving of ourselves in the service of others. Many times, we think we are just helping, but in many cases, we are helping ourselves when we serve. For example, we may have had a really rough day and the last thing we want to do is help someone else. Yet, we struggle through it, not recognizing that when we do, we also benefit.

Those who serve are doing the hands and feet work of the church. We are the catalysts for how others see the church that we represent. A first-time visitor's future involvement with the church can either be established or broken during that very first encounter at the front door. A greeter with a bad attitude could turn someone in need away. An unhelpful guest services person might hinder another from participating in an upcoming event, but a positive interaction opens many doors.

One of the other key factors to serving is how the church appreciates those who do serve. A thankful church will always attract more help than a church that expects much, but lacks in the area of thankfulness. It doesn't take much to say, "Thank you for your help." It not only shows appreciation, but it encourages others to volunteer again, to become even more involved in the various ministries taking place inside the church.

❧

PRAYER

An Unknown Need

May the Lord provide for a need you didn't know you had.

> *"Therefore I say unto you, Take no thought for your life, what ye shall eat, or what ye shall drink; nor yet for your body, what ye shall put on. Is not the life more than meat, and the body than raiment? Behold the fowls of the air: for they sow not, neither do they reap, nor gather into barns; yet your heavenly Father feedeth them. Are ye not much better than they"* (Matthew 6:25-26).

Gracious Walk

CHAPTER 27

Trust Him and His Promises

It is truly a crazy thing, that no matter how amazing your week or weekend is, your mind or the enemy has a way of casting a shadow upon it. Let me share activities from this past weekend:

- Attended a Christmas Event at Mrs. Kerry's church.

- Attended a Men's God Encounter at church and experienced the joy of watching men bond with other men in the presence of our Lord.

- Blessed an amazing man of God with concert tickets.

- Cried during the men's encounter for a man whom I didn't know, but had heard earlier in the day that he was removed from the church under the suspicion of being a witch. Clearly there are more details to the story of which I'm not privy, but for some reason it bothered me deeply and I wept for him.

- Helped baptize some men from the "God

Encounter" on Sunday morning.

- Invited Ms. B to a concert with me in a couple weeks and she accepted.

- Marq gave me a rubber ring which says, "I am man" on one side and on the other the Bible reference, "Proverbs 18:22." That scripture, which was not actually written word-for-word on the bracelet is, "He who finds a wife finds a good thing, and obtains favor from the LORD." (NKJV)

- Met two awesome souls on Friday night while out to dinner, Ms. B and Ms. L. Yes, I'm into first initials only. It was great company and great conversation. We laughed and bantered most of the evening and then went for dessert at Eddie V's in Orlando.

- Received an awesome, housewarming gift from Ms. Lydia.

- Sir Maximo attended church. You could tell he was touched, as he hadn't attended a church service in a long time. I even had lunch with him afterwards.

Now anyone looking at my past weekend events would surely say, "You had a great weekend my friend," but in my mind I began to feel guilty, guilty because I felt like I was cheating on a friend I dated for a short period, but hadn't seen in over a month. I'd recently met another woman and after several dates, I invited her to a concert. Yet at the time, she has been the desire of my heart and always on my mind. I even had prayers before the Lord about her. The moment I asked this new lady out, I felt a level of stress and wrongness. Right or wrong in my thoughts, I felt a level of guilt.

I began to question and second guess all the things I believe I had heard from the Lord over the last month or so. All the things I felt He had me do I began to question. Was I no longer willing to wait for the promise? Did I hear what I just wanted to hear during my prayers? Had I just decided it had been long enough? Was I overreacting as I did ask the Lord for someone to attend the concert with? My thoughts were just running rampant.

At the end of the evening, I got home and walked up and down the block in front of my home talking with Lord. I went inside, showered and still felt the need for more time in the Lord's presence. In my closet, upon my knees, I prayed. Then I began to calm myself and remember who I was. I'm a child of the God, a member of the chosen generation, part of a holy nation. Greater is He who is in me, and I am blessed in all that I do. I remembered, or should say, I was enlightened to trust in Him.

Although I have to admit, I was fine for a short period. But the mind or the enemy can be a powerful voice inside of our heads. We can, at times, repeat over and over that which is bothering us. I went to bed feeling that level of stress again and tossed and turned all night. Around 2:30 am I was up and upon my knees again. Needing that spiritual strengthening, but this time, after praying, I felt a level of peace that has remained. I'm no longer stressing or worrying. I (we) walk in faith. That is where this morning I stand. I walk in faith and place my trust in the Lord that whichever way He guides me will be better than anything I could think of or plan myself. Indeed, if we trust in the Lord and walk in faith, all the other stuff that comes into our mind or the enemy whispers we can ignore. Our Lord is indeed in control and we walk in faith and place 100% of our trust in Him.

─·✾·─

INSPIRATIONAL THOUGHT
Who God Has Planned for You

The woman God has planned for you may not be 36-24-36. The man God has planned for you may not be rich, but they will have exactly what you need for agape love and happiness.

> *"Whoso findeth a wife findeth a good thing, and obtaineth favour of the Lord"*
> (Proverbs 18:22).

CHAPTER 28

A Blessed Day Indeed!

What an absolutely intense Sunday, but I wouldn't have it any other way. The day was filled with a morning church service, an adopted-family Christmas-gift wrapping-party, a Marriott associates Christmas event and finally a Marriott post-Christmas party get-together. What started at 7:00 am with prayer ended at roughly 10:30 pm. Indeed, a long day, but each activity had its own adventure.

Church service began with the pastoral morning group prayer in the prayer room. There is something special and awesome to hear men and women of God praying aloud all at the same time, all of them speaking in tongues, having been baptized by the Holy Spirit. Typically my prayer time would be in a place of silence and privacy. It took me many months to get accustomed to group prayer, but the Lord taught me how to embrace the moment and enjoy the power of group prayer. When I'm in the room with all the pastors and occasionally some members of the congregation, I think on the scripture, *"Again I say unto you, That if two of you shall agree on earth as touching any thing that they shall ask, it shall be done for them of my Father which is in heaven"* (Matthew 18:19). Now, I look forward to the Sunday morning prayer gathering. Just knowing my prayers are bundled with the prayers of others is comforting (even when I don't actually know what they are praying about, as most are praying in tongues and others are singing in a lower voice).

Sunday morning church services ended early for me as we didn't have any baptisms to do, so I quietly exited stage left around 10:30. (No, I wasn't actually on a stage, it is an old school saying about leaving a place or sneaking out / smile).

Up next was the "Second Annual Holiday with a Purpose" event, hosted by my cousin Nicole—an event in honor of her father who passed in 2017. He had a heart for giving unto others and this is her way of keeping his charitable works alive. What I didn't know when she invited me to participate was that I would be the only man in attendance among roughly twenty women, mostly teachers. That year she had adopted five kids, some homeless (i.e. living in hotels) and others with varying home challenges and struggles.

We all had previously picked a child and purchased gifts in advance. I really didn't know all the details once again. I didn't know, when I agreed to help, that each child had a number of people who had also picked him or her. So the gift blessing per child was tremendous. For two hours we wrapped gifts. Actually, they wrapped gifts while I stuffed my face with food and picked at folks for their horrible gift wrapping skills. I will admit, I was humbled during the event when asked to offer the prayer. The Lord was indeed with us as the prayer just rolled off my tongue. I was in awe.

I stayed until I received a text message from BiBi (my future wife) to come to a Marriott Associate Christmas party. First thought, more food and fun. I'm all about free food. I arrived, entered the ballroom and was blown away by this extravaganza. Driving over, my initial thought was this was going to be a small event. I wasn't expecting hundreds of Marriott associates and their family members. Food, balloons, gift giveaways, a cartoonist, and a DJ. I walked in and the Wobble song was playing as folk in mass were dancing. Now this is how all companies should acknowledge the hard work their employees do throughout the year.

The Lord blessed me as a child with an openness to talk with anyone. Actually, I think I have some type of personality trait that opens the hearts of others and people will just share their troubles, their struggles, and their dreams in life. Being a person who will talk with anyone, I got into a conversation with a lady in a wheelchair. She was in line to get herself a custom-made balloon. We laughed about all the out-of-control kids running rampant throughout the place, but it was all in jest. I walked away from the conversation to get a coffee and on my return, I saw this thing that looked like a honeycomb, and it was really dripping honey. I stood there in amazement. I grew up in Detroit and had never seen a honeycomb (no, I don't get out of the house a lot, so don't judge me / smile). There was a lady standing there with a fork and I asked, "What do I eat that with?" She responded, "Just like it is."

So being the bougie man I am, I got a fork and a dinner plate, I stuck the fork in the honeycomb and broke off a piece. I headed over to the table and, oh, my goodness, it was so good. I even shared it with the lady in the wheelchair, as she was still waiting in line. What I wasn't expecting was the wax portion to stick to my teeth.

Moments later I saw everything on the table falling off because the table cloth had wrapped itself around the lady's wheelchair wheel and she was moving on, at first, not realizing the problem. Clearly, she looked distraught as everyone began to stare. I had one question for her, *"What do you owe me?"* She said, *"My apology."* I said, *"Nope!"* She said, *"Thank you, Lord."* I said, *"Nope!"* as that response was shocking. She asked, *"What do I owe you?"* and I said, *"Another plate with honey on it"* and we both laughed it off.

About thirty minutes later, I'm picking at Bibi about giving away her balloon to a little girl who saw it, and the lady pulls up in her wheelchair with a plate, two forks and honey. We all just laughed. She had fulfilled her apology quest. What I didn't know until attending the after Christmas party event, was that one of the Marriott workers had seen the entire event and was unable to assist. I saw him later and he asked if I was the man who helped. He went on to say how seeing my act of assisting impacted him. Here is the key, we never know how one selfless act in helping another may touch the heart of someone else. This man was really emotional about the whole thing. We always have an opportunity to turn a sad situation into an opportunity to bless.

It is important that we remember what Jesus said about the hypocrisy of the Pharisees, *"Therefore whatever they tell you to observe, that observe and do, but do not do according to their works; for they say, and do not do. For they bind heavy burdens, hard to bear, and lay them on men's shoulders; but they themselves will not move them with one of their fingers. But all their works they do to be seen by men. They make their phylacteries broad and enlarge the borders of their garments. They love the best places at feasts, the best seats in the synagogues, greetings in the marketplaces, and to be called by men, 'Rabbi, Rabbi.'"* (Matthew 23:3-7 NKJV). When we act out of the kindness of our hearts, we are behaving like godly men and women. We are reaching out our hands to be a blessing in the lives of others. When doing an ARK (Act of Random Kindness), let it be from your heart and not for the visual appreciation of another. *"The king will reply, 'Truly*

When we act out of the kindness of our hearts, we are behaving like godly men and women.

I tell you, whatever you did for one of the least of these brothers and sisters of mine, you did for me.'" (Matthew 25:40 NIV)

─╲╱─

INSPIRATIONAL THOUGHT

Don't Make Things Difficult!

Gentle acts of kindness can have the biggest rewards.

CHAPTER 29

Always Wear the Armor of God

Occasionally, I run across something that just makes me think or say, "Why would anybody do such a thing"? I am talking about something that breaks your heart. For the life of me, I have no idea why anybody would go out and have an image of a demonic spirit tattooed on his neck appearing to whisper into his ear. Lots of questions and no immediate answers. I know we all go through struggles in life, but why would any man want to place a large tattoo of a red-colored demon with horns on his body even in the worst times of tribulation or struggles in life? I was just stunned by it.

I'm not judging anyone who has a tattoo, as I have one on my thigh. It's a shark with a torn cloth in its mouth. I got it after becoming a certified scuba diver. In this young man's case, all I could think of was, "He's wearing the wrong thing." (not in the sense of attire, but his spiritual covering). So, I pulled out my Bible and in the very first section I opened, I ran across the passage on the full armor of God. I want to remind you that every morning when you arise, and before you leave the house, you need to do this:

As it is written, *"Finally, my brethren, be strong in the Lord, and in the power of his might. Put on the whole armour of God, that ye may be able to stand against the wiles of the devil. For we wrestle not against flesh and blood, but against principalities, against powers, against the rulers of the darkness of this world, against spiritual wickedness in high places. Wherefore take unto you the whole armour of God, that ye may be able to withstand in the evil day, and having done all, to stand. Stand therefore, having your loins girt about with truth, and having on the breastplate of righteousness; and your feet shod with the preparation of the gospel of peace; above all, taking the shield of faith, wherewith ye shall be able to quench all the fiery darts of the wicked. And take the helmet of salvation, and the sword of the Spirit, which is the word of God. Praying always with all prayer and supplication in the Spirit, and watching thereunto with all perseverance and supplication for all saints"* (Ephesians 6:10-18).

Life is already full of struggles; why darken your day with the ominous image of an evil spirit speaking into your mind? Whispering in your ear all day? Leading and directing your behavior and actions? That is not the life Jesus died in your behalf to give you. That is not the life our Lord God desires for you. That is not the life we obtain when we are filled with the Holy Spirit. You and I are not supposed to be of this world. Remember Jesus said concerning His disciples, *"They are not of the world, even as I am not of the world. Sanctify them through thy truth: thy word is truth"* (John 17:16-17).

You don't let the enemy whisper in your ear all day long. You definitely don't tattoo a demonic image on your body. As written in the Word of God (2 Corinthians 10:3-5 NKJV), *"Though we walk in the flesh, we do not war according to the flesh. For the weapons of our warfare are not carnal but mighty in God for pulling down strongholds, casting down arguments and every high thing that exalts itself against the knowledge of God, bringing every thought into captivity to the obedience of Christ."* Also, Revelation 12:11 speaks of the weaponry with which Christians fight the enemy (Satan and his demonic followers): *"And they overcame him by the blood of the Lamb, and by the word of their testimony; and they loved not their lives unto the death."* You don't have to bear that burden. You have armor that you can put on every single day and superior weapons to fight with as you battle the enemy and protect yourself.

I would love to personally meet that man one day. I would love to tell him of the love of God and the better road that he can walk. I would love to tell him how Jesus will speak to his heart every day and lead him into a valuable and fruitful life. I wonder what made him do that, what damaging experiences he has had in life. I might ask, "Why, why would you do such a thing?" but I wouldn't leave it there. I would encourage him to believe in the cross and I would definitely offer to pray for him that he might encounter the One who said, "I am the way, the truth, and the life" (John 14:6). Come to think of it, I don't think I would even bring up his tattoo in a conversation. A "gracious walk" is all about giving grace to people who need it, who are unworthy, who have made bad choices in their lives, who are hurting and trying to compensate for it. I would just try to be as gracious and as kind as I could with him, and maybe that would help him make positive decisions to change his life in a positive way. Loving concern always helps more than harsh criticism.

~\|/~

PRAYER

Spiritual Deliverance

Lord, we pray for all those who on a daily basis live under the whisper of the enemy in their ear. Lord, we ask that You break that demonic hold on their lives and set them free. For the Word of God says, *"If the Son therefore shall make you free, ye shall be free indeed"* (John 8:36). In Jesus' mighty name we pray, Amen.

CHAPTER 30

Opportunities to Share the Good News

"When we align ourselves with the Lord, he makes a way for us to see open doors of opportunity." (Pastor Torress / an email to me)

The above quote is so very true and lays out a clear path to understanding, in some ways, why things happen in our lives as we fill this role of being the hands and feet of the Lord. Opportunities just seem to present themselves. The Word says, *"Preach the word; be instant in season, out of season; reprove, rebuke, exhort with all long suffering and doctrine"* (2 Timothy 4:2). We must be ready to share the good news of Jesus however the occasion presents itself and wherever it does.

I tend to always have on my wrist the little rubber bracelets with Bible verses written on them. I sometimes feel like a walking rubber bank, but I'll be doggone, those bracelets will start a discussion in some odd places. I was flying in recently from Grand Cayman after a short vacation. I was standing in line waiting to get through customs and a lady next to me saw one of the bracelets and made a comment to me about it, So I pulled it off and handed it to her. She was just overjoyed. That little piece of rubber was just an accessory to me, but it brightened her day and all those with her as they looked at it. It was just enough time to say, "God Bless You" and share the Word of God.

I was in the mall right before the Christmas holidays, waiting for some packages to get wrapped. I had about thirty minutes to waste and was standing in the lady's shoe department in awe and shock. I thought my daughter might like a pair of shoes for Christmas, thus my awe and shock. Have you seen the price of women's shoes? Oh, my goodness, I was blown away. Just about the time I returned to my senses, a young sale associate walks over and asked if she could provide any assistance? I responded, *"No I'm good, just looking."* Didn't want to let her know my price bewilderment. Surprisingly, she asked about one of the rubber bracelets on my arm. I told her about the one that denotes the need to put on the armor of God. She smiled and I reached down, pulled it off and handed it to her. She said, *"I was just asking God for a sign."* We chatted for a bit and then I left to get my wrapped gifts and head home.

About three weeks later I was again back there to have some additional packages wrapped, and I saw this young lady again. I stopped and we began to chat. I asked, *"Did you receive the sign you were seeking?"* That led to the most amazing conversation. She began to share a recent injury she received when falling through an attic ceiling, the surgeries she had, and constant pain she is in. The sign was that she needed to wear her spiritual armor as the warfare by the enemy was against her. We talked for the longest time about the goodness and healing power of our Lord. Even though we don't always understand His timing concerning healing, we walk in faith.

This is why it is so important to be ready to share the goodness of Jesus at any time. We never know when an opportunity to be a blessing to another will present itself. Today, Evelyn and I are email friends. She is on my distribution list of inspirational messages and on my prayer list for healing. As I told her, "I don't know when God will heal you of this issue, but He will be glorified and you now have a testimony to share with others." Here is the other cool part of this story. My jeweler is also in that same mall and she also, a few years ago, fell through her ceiling, resulting in many of the same injuries. The Lord healed her and I put these two ladies in touch with each other. Now they can share their walk and provide comfort to each other. God is good, all the time.

It is so important to be ready to share the goodness of Jesus at any time.

—⁄—

INSPIRATIONAL THOUGHT

You Are Needed

Be a blessing. Buy someone a coffee, a meal, give a hug, lend a helping hand, or just an open ear with a closed mouth. Somebody needs you today.

> *"For I was an hungred, and ye gave me meat: I was thirsty, and ye gave me drink: I was a stranger, and ye took me in: Naked, and ye clothed me: I was sick, and ye visited me: I was in prison, and ye came unto me. Then shall the righteous answer him, saying, Lord, when saw we thee an hungred, and fed thee? or thirsty, and gave thee drink? When saw we thee a stranger, and took thee in? or naked, and clothed thee? Or when saw we thee sick, or in prison, and came unto thee? And the King shall answer and say unto them, Verily I say unto you, Inasmuch as ye have done it unto one of the least of these my brethren, ye have done it unto me"* (Matthew 25:35-40).

CHAPTER 31

Inspirational Thoughts

DO YOU KNOW HIM

I walk in faith. I marvel at His inspiration and confirmation. I stand in awe of things He does. Do you know Him?

> *"Jesus answered, "I am the way and the truth and the life. No one comes to the Father except through me"* (John 14:6 NIV).

HOLY SPIRIT LEAD

When the Holy Spirit leads you to do a thing, just do it! Don't try to figure it out! Just ACT! Knowing deep in your heart and spirit, a need existed and the work will never be in vain.

> *"For there are three that bear record in heaven, the Father, the Word, and the Holy Ghost: and these three are one"* (1 John 5:7).

BE OBEDIENT, MOVE WHEN INSTRUCTED

When the Lord instructs you to act, you move right then without hesitation.

"Now if you obey me fully and keep my covenant, then out of all nations you will be my treasured possession" (Exodus 19:5 NIV).

HUG ME DAILY

Give your loved ones a hug and kiss today. Remind them of how special/important they are in your life. Tomorrow isn't guaranteed.

"We love him, because he first loved us" (1 John 4:19).

MAKE YOURSELF LAUGH

There are days I make myself laugh. I was texting with a friend today and remembering how we continue to lift each other up. Over and over. Then I imagined we found ourselves in heaven. God asks, "What are you two doing here? Your house is not ready yet." I respond, "We've been lifting each other up for years, and then, BAM, here we are." God looks, shakes his head, and says, "That's not how this works." Then the five of us have a good laugh.

"He will yet fill your mouth with laughter and your lips with shouts of joy" (Job 8:21 NIV).

SPIRITUAL FOOD

So many people are in need of spiritual food. Humbled, I can offer a snack, knowing the Lord has a banquet ready.

"Therefore, rid yourselves of all malice and all deceit, hypocrisy, envy, and slander of every kind. Like newborn babies, crave pure spiritual milk, so that by it you may grow up in your salvation, now that you have tasted that the Lord is good" (1 Peter 2:1-3 NIV).

DATE NIGHT

When was the last time you and your love had one? Spending quality time improves communication and builds intimacy.

"Let him kiss me with the kisses of his mouth: for thy love is better than wine"
(Song of Solomon 1:2).

THE LORD IS NEVER LATE

He's always right on time. Prayed about a blessing before me. Didn't hear a "No," thus I moved forward. Then right before shelling out the cash, He intervened and killed the deal. A gentle intervention before revealing what I hadn't thought about. A better blessing opportunity is forthcoming indeed.

"But I trusted in thee, O LORD: I said, Thou art my God. My times are in thy hand: deliver me from the hand of mine enemies, and from them that persecute me. Make thy face to shine upon thy servant: save me for thy mercies' sake" (Psalms 31:14-16).

"Behold, O God our shield, and look upon the

face of thine anointed. For a day in thy courts is better than a thousand. I had rather be a doorkeeper in the house of my God, than to dwell in the tents of wickedness. For the Lord God is a sun and shield: the Lord will give grace and glory: no good thing will he withhold from them that walk uprightly. O Lord of hosts, blessed is the man that trusteth in thee" (Psalms 84:9-12).

SO YOU'VE BEEN SUCCESSFUL WITHOUT GOD

So, you've been successful by your own hands and arms, without God. How successful would have you have been with God?

"Observe what the Lord your God requires: Walk in obedience to him, and keep his decrees and commands, his laws and regulations, as written in the Law of Moses. Do this so that you may prosper in all you do and wherever you go" (1 Kings 2:3 NIV).

DELIGHT IN THE LORD

Delight in the Lord and rebuke the conversations full of vulgarity, racial division, and false conspiracy theories.

"Ye are of God, little children, and have overcome them: because greater is he that is in you, than he that is in the world" (1 John 4:4).

Be vigilant, tender of heart, and protect those weaker than you. Rise up, bless someone, and have an amazing day!

SAD NEWS DOESN'T NEED MORE SAD NEWS

When someone shares sad news with you, the last thing they need to hear is a similar sad story. Be a blessing! Anoint them with oil! Speak words of positivity and prayer!

> *"Is any among you afflicted? let him pray. Is any merry? let him sing psalms. Is any sick among you? let him call for the elders of the church; and let them pray over him, anointing him with oil in the name of the Lord: And the prayer of faith shall save the sick, and the Lord shall raise him up; and if he have committed sins, they shall be forgiven him. Confess your faults one to another, and pray one for another, that ye may be healed. The effectual fervent prayer of a righteous man availeth much"* (James 5:13-16).

PRAYER DIVIDENDS

Sometimes folks just make you laugh. One of the cooks at Bob Evans yelled at me one morning, "Hey church man, please pray for me because I'm about to hurt someone in here." All my Bible reading here in this restaurant is paying "prayer" dividends.

"So then faith cometh by hearing, and hearing by the word of God" (Romans 10:17).

THOSE ASSIGNED TO YOU

I heard Pastor Marvin Jackson say one time, "Those assigned to you can't leave and those who are not, can't stay."

BE CAREFUL HOW YOU TREAT OTHERS

Another one of my favorite quotes from Pastor Marvin Jackson is, "Don't treat trash like treasure and treasure like trash."

BREATH IN OUR LUNGS

I heard my friend, Megan Lopez-Abdullahi, share one of her favorite quotes one time, "If He blesses us with breath in the morning, then we're on the right track."

LOVE HARD

"Don't be afraid. Go ahead and give your heart. Love hard and with all that you are. Tomorrow is not promised. Love is in your DNA!

"Whereas ye know not what shall be on the morrow. For what is your life? It is even a vapour, that appeareth for a little time, and then vanisheth away" (James 4:14).

WITHOUT LIMITS

Don't you dare let someone else's limited thoughts cause you to set boundaries on God's blessings and plans for your life.

"Now unto him that is able to do exceeding abundantly above all that we ask or think, according to the power that worketh in us" (Ephesians 3:20).

OUR OWN JUDAS

I had a great conversation last night on how for a reason and a season people enter our lives. I think even an occasional Judas can come into our lives, not to lead toward death, but to glorify God in how we handle issues that deceived person creates. Yet I have to wonder, What if I'm the Judas in someone's life? It didn't work out too well for him. I am determined not to fill this role.

"The thief cometh not, but for to steal, and to kill, and to destroy: I am come that they might have life, and that they might have it more abundantly" (John 10:10).

BE A SERVANT

Never skip an opportunity to serve. You'll see God move in awesome ways. He keeps me in awe.

"God is not unjust; he will not forget your work and the love you have shown him as you

have helped his people and continue to help
them" (Hebrews 6:10 NIV).

BEING A BLESSING ISN'T EXPENSIVE

Being a blessing doesn't have to cost a penny.
That thing you're in a rush to do will be there. The
time you give to another is more precious than gold.

> *"But this I say, He which soweth sparingly*
> *shall reap also sparingly; and he which soweth*
> *bountifully shall reap also bountifully. Every*
> *man according as he purposeth in his heart,*
> *so let him give; not grudgingly, or of necessity:*
> *for God loveth a cheerful giver"*
> (2 Corinthians 9:6-8).

MARRIAGE BUILT UPON
A STRONG FOUNDATION

Build your marriage and relationships on the firm
foundation of Jesus Christ. When the hurricanes of
life come, you will bend and sway, but your godly
relationships won't fall apart. Lord, help us all see
the strength of building everything upon You.

> *"Therefore whosoever heareth these sayings of*
> *mine, and doeth them, I will liken him unto a*
> *wise man, which built his house upon a rock:*
> *And the rain descended, and the floods came,*
> *and the winds blew, and beat upon that house;*
> *and it fell not: for it was founded upon a rock.*
> *And every one that heareth these sayings of*

mine, and doeth them not, shall be likened unto a foolish man, which built his house upon the sand: And the rain descended, and the floods came, and the winds blew, and beat upon that house; and it fell: and great was the fall of it" (Matthew 7:24-27).

SEPARATED IS STILL MARRIED

Separated is still "married." What part of their hearts can he or she honestly offer? Pray for that wayward person and then run.

"Thou shalt not commit adultery"
(Exodus 20:14).

Gracious Walk

CHAPTER 32

Acts of Random Kindness (ARK)

BE A BLESSING!
Thanksgiving Idea

It took just a moment this morning in prayer to think of someone who might be alone tomorrow on Thanksgiving Day. If you have an empty dinner seat or can make room for one more, reach out, break bread with them, and feel the presence of God.

BE A BLESSING!
Christmas Idea

Time for our 12 Days of Christmas activity. I believe this would be year five of our Acts of Random Kindness (ARK). This year my request of you will be a little different. The necessity still exists to be a blessing unto others, but I feel a more pressing thing this year is needed. Did you know the *"Spirit also helpeth our infirmities: for we know not what we should pray for as we ought: but the Spirit itself maketh intercession for us with groanings which cannot be uttered"* (Romans 8:26). How awesome is that knowledge!

So, many people are in need of renewed hope, forgiveness, improved lives, healing, and a stirring of their spirits. This year, instead of participating in ARK, pray for those in need. It is written in Psalms 54:2, *"Hear my prayer, O God; give ear to the words of my mouth."* So I'm asking you pick twelve individuals and each day beginning (enter date 12 days before Christmas) pray for them each day until Christmas. Let the relationship you have with God be a blessing to someone else. As the Spirit intercedes for you, you can intercede for someone else.

I ask that you join me this year in praying for others as I pray for you. Together we can make a difference and have an impact, even if we never see the results with our own eyes. Be a Blessing! Someone Needs You Today.

BE A BLESSING!
Easter Idea

Forget the fancy dress and the big hat. Leave the yellow suit and matching shoes in the closet. Introduce someone to the Lord by inviting him or her to church on Easter. You'll get all the "real" attention you'll ever need.

BE A BLESSING!
Who Needs You Today

God does so much for us, can't we do just a little something for someone else?

BE A BLESSING!

Three Difficult Days Each Year

Christmas, Mother's Day and Valentine's Day can be difficult times for some people. On these days, as you should with the other 362 days in the year, show some love for others. Call someone and just say, "Hi." Let others know you are thinking of them.

BE A BLESSING!

Setting Right Priorities

Nice car, huge bank accounts, lovely home and beautiful clothes you may have, none of which can be taken to the grave. I'll take the priceless love of God. The hugs from my loving spouse. The helping hand toward someone in need. The hope and prayers for myself, family and you for eternal life.

BE A BLESSING!

Easy Blessing Opportunities

- Always keep gift cards in your wallets in varying amounts from local stores and restaurants. They are perfect and timely blessing gifts.

- Hold a door for someone walking behind you, even if they aren't close to the door. Don't expect a thank you.

- Be a listener even if it means you have to stop what you're doing.

- You've just entered the no texting and email zone. Touch someone's heart with a personal message written in a card. Then mail it. Yes, get a stamp and mail it.

- Down to your last three dollars, buy someone in need a coffee. Yes, you'll be broke, unable to buy something off the dollar menu, but you'll be emotionally wealthy.

- Visit the local Dollar Store and make homeless Ziploc care bags. Fill them with hygiene products and goodies. Keep them always in your car. There is always someone in need.

- During the winter months, stop by a local Salvation Army store and buy gloves, knit hats and scarves. Keep them in your car and pass them out when you see someone in need.

- When the Lord says, "Give that person all you have in your pocket," don't hesitate.

- Take one for the team – when the spouse/kids make a request of you and you'd rather do something different, take one for the team (spouse or children). Nothing is more important than God and then your family.

BE A BLESSING!

Server at Church

Yes, life is difficult. Yes, it can be a real struggle. Yes, you've have a tough time recently. Yes, some folks seem to just have everything. Are we done now with your "misery moment"? Life can't be too bad. You have a cell, you're on FB, and you're still alive; now go serve at church.

BE A BLESSING!
Dementia and Alzheimer's

It is not our loved ones' fault dementia or Alzheimer's has overcome them. Today, let us have more patience, show love, and spend time talking with them about the good times we've had together in the past.

BLESSING AWARENESS!
Let Him Be Him

Ladies, you wanted a godly man. God blessed you with one. Let him be one. Let him serve you the way he wants to serve and love you.

BLESSING AWARENESS!
Let Her Be Her

Fellas, you wanted a godly woman. God blessed you with one. Now keep doing everything you did to win her heart. If she likes standing in your personal space, ask her to stand even closer. Worship with her. Pray for and over her.

WORKS CITED

Chapman, Gary D. *The 5 Love Languages.* Chicago, IL, Northfield Publishing, 2008.

Evans, David G. *Dare to Be a Man: The Truth Every Man Must Know … and Every Woman Needs to Know about Him.* New York, NY, G. P. Putnam Sons, 2009.

Feldhahn, Shaunti. *For Men Only – A Straightforward Guide to the Inner Lives of Women.* Atlanta, GA, Multnomah Books, 2006.

Franklin, Kirk. *The Blueprint: A Plan for Living Above Life's Storms.* New York, NY, Penguin Group, 2010.

Jackson, Marvin, pastor. "Inspirational." Chosen Generation Ministries, Good Life Broadcasting, 2018

Meyer, Joyce. "Inspirational." *Everyday Life*, Super Channel, 2018.

Osteen, Joel. *Become a Better You: 7 Keys to Improving Your Life Every Day.* New York, NY, Simon & Schuster, 2007.

Teddy Pendergrass. *"When Somebody Loves You Back."* Life Is A Song Worth Living, June 2, 1978. https://genius.com/Teddy-pendergrass-when-somebody-loves-you-back-lyrics.

Zacharias, Ravi. *Has Christianity Failed You.* Grand Rapids, MI, Wolgemuth and Associates, 2010.